Everything Flowers

Quilts from the Garden

Jean & Valori Wells

C&T PUBLISHING

©Copyright 1996
Jean and Valori Wells

Developmental Editor:
Barbara Konzak Kuhn

Technical Editor:
Sally Lanzarotti

Book Design & Illustration:
Jill K. Berry

Flower photography by
Valori Wells.

Quilt photography by
Ross Chandler, Bend, Oregon.

Library of Congress Cataloging-in-Publication

Wells, Jean.
    Everything Flowers: quilts from the garden / Jean and Valori Wells.
        p.   cm.
    ISBN 1-57120-007-X (pbk.)
    1. Patchwork—Patterns.
    2. Appliqué—Patterns.
    3. Patchwork quilts. 4. Flowers in art. I. Wells, Valori. II. Title.
    TT835.W4647 1996
    746.46—dc20
                            95-46494

Published by C&T Publishing
P.O. Box 1456
Lafayette, California 94549

Printed in Hong Kong
10 9 8 7 6 5 4 3 2 1

Acknowledgements

Catherine in her garden

Where would the book be without the flower gardens that inspire us? Our thanks to the following people for their gardens, and their kindness: Phyllis Smith let us photograph her perennial garden at her nursery, Eastside Gardens. Conklin's Guest House in Sisters, Oregon, provided the perfect setting for the poppy fields photograph. Many of the wildflowers shown are from Catherine and Mel Bryan's garden. Catherine and I paddled Valori around a pond in a canoe so she could get the perfect photographs. Thank you Catherine for all of your assistance and suggestions.

I would like to thank my students, the Garden Girls, who created some of the beautiful and innovative quilts for *Everything Flowers.* We helped each other through tough spots: sharing fabric that was needed, suggesting changes when viewing the subject matter, or simply encouraging each other. The Garden Girls are Marrell Dickson, Kathy Blair, Ruth Golden Ingham, Cindy Uttley, Phyllis Smith, and Diane Rupp.

Jackie Erickson and Lawry Thorn were invaluable in stitching blocks together and helping machine quilt the various quilts. Jackie and Lawry also gave encouragement and helped in some of the decision-making when it came to auditioning fabrics.

It is truly a pleasure to be doing another book with C&T Publishing. I was very excited to have Barbara Konzak Kuhn assigned as the developmental editor. Barbara is efficient as well as visionary, which is rare. Sally Lanzarotti has the patience to check and recheck every little technical detail. Diane Pedersen has worked with me on almost every C&T book. I value her expert "design eye," insight, and creative vision when it comes to book design. My appreciation goes out to her. And finally, thank you Todd and Tony Hensley for believing in the project and running such a fine publishing house as C&T Publishing.

Table of Contents

Introduction

The joys of gardening are much like the joys of quilting. Both are a process of taking raw materials and creating a thoughtful and beautiful work that develops over time. Quilts and gardens start with ideas and dreams. A palette of fabric or a tray of bedding plants sets the tone for the creative process. A plan is established and parameters are set. A quilter starts with an idea and decides the mood of the quilt—should the fabric colors be soft and misty, giving the impression of early morning light, or will they be dramatic, dark, rich colors? Should the quilt be pieced or appliquéd, or a combination of both? After many decisions are made, the quilter cuts the fabric from the palette, then arranges and rearranges the pieces to carry out the idea. A gardener follows the same process using a visual picture of how the plants will look when mature. The palette consists of seeds or bedding plants. The plants are arranged by the amount of space they need to grow, the height they will become, their color, and their shape. Both the gardener and the quilter will think about color placement in the overall composition. They ask, "Is there enough contrast to make the shapes interesting? Is there enough movement in the composition to make it interesting? Is there an accent? Is there something that is brighter, lighter, or darker that makes the composition 'sing'?" Nurturing is also a necessary part of the process and is self-fulfilling. If you pay attention to details and take care during the construction, the results are often perfect. Whether it be a finished quilt hanging in a quilt show or a gift of pressed flowers or dried herbs, the commitment in achieving the end results sweetens the rewards of the harvest.

Everything Flowers has been created with the quilter in mind…it is a bridge for creating one-of-a-kind quilts and floral crafts with flowers as the inspiration. Gardening and quilting have become very interlocked in my life. With my daughter, Valori, as my helper, I started the *Daisies* quilt using flowers as a design source. I learned from her how to "transition" from one color area to another. Years ago Valori became very interested in flower gardening. Not only has she developed perennial and herb gardens, but flowers have also become her source of inspiration in her college studies at Pacific Northwest College of Art. I have watched her use flowers to design wonderful prints, sculpture, photographs, and graphics. Valori designed the *Wildflowers* quilt using hand-dyed fabrics. She makes me see my fabrics differently. Normally, I tend to be very literal and only see what is in a print, but through her I can

see the full potential of a print. Valori worked extensively with me on this book. While I would visualize gardens, decorative accents, and the quilt projects, she would focus on ideas "from the garden," the page layouts, and the photography. We collaborated on the design of the book, with both of us designing the quilts.

You will see from the projects in the book that flowers have truly been an inspiration. Even if growing your own garden isn't possible, you can purchase flowers, arrange them in a vase, enjoy them, and then use them for other flower related projects. *Everything Flowers* is meant to be your garden of ideas and inspiration.

Enjoy!

Chapter 1

The Creative Process

Creativity is an experience that starts deep within us. It is a positive flow of energy that builds and grows as it develops. When we open ourselves to the process, we open ourselves to our own creativity. By involving ourselves in the creative process, we in turn nurture our own abilities. It is truly like planting a seed in soil, and then watering, weeding, and fertilizing until the plant matures.

The purpose of this book is to present ways in which to put your floral dreams and impressions into a quilt. Using flowers, which are a very familiar and comforting subject matter, will give you confidence to try a new process. Once you develop confidence in new ways of working, the ideas will flow from you. You may feel ineffective in tapping your own creative juices. Maybe you are unsure how to approach the process. Perhaps you have ideas or dreams, but can't actualize them or put them into practice. Draw on your present knowledge and traditions. Use the skills and abilities you've developed in your quilting adventures. Traditional quilts are the foundation, or comfort zone, from which to spring. Use traditional quilts as a bridge to more innovative designs.

Creative Discovery

As creative quiltmakers, we need to learn to be self-nourishing. We must consciously replenish our creative resources as we use them. It is similar to fishing: If you don't give the fishing hole a rest, or restock the pond, all the fish will be gone. "Stocking the pond," so to speak, requires the active pursuit of new ideas, whether shopping for new fabrics, attending a quilt show, taking a class, or taking a quiet afternoon for reflection. I am an intense person, especially when I am working on a new project. I like to get things done exactly as planned, and on time. However, I find that after a while I need a break. My husband and I will go to the beach, or play golf. As I distance myself from past deadlines, I start to relax. Soon my mind frees itself from the routine. I observe my new surroundings: the textures of weathered wood on an old barn, a field of daisies, the architectural details of a building, or a beautiful sunset. I am restocking the pond.

Keep a journal with you in case you want to make notes to yourself. One time, John and I were driving to a football game and I suddenly started resolving some design problems. But, I could not find a single piece of paper in the car. We stopped and John bought me a notepad—I busily jotted down ideas for the next hour. Since my drawing abilities are minimal, I scribble notes or make funny sketches. I describe how things look, or how something makes me feel, even if I can't draw it. One of my favorite authors and illustrators is Sara Midda. In her book, *In and Out of the Garden*, she captures her impressions of gardening in wonderful watercolor sketches and presents valuable information. Her books are garden journals with an artist's touch (see Bibliography on page 96).

Creativity is born out of observation and attention to detail. Once an idea is generated, getting in touch with yourself and your own resources is the key to the process. The power of observation is an asset to design. Teach yourself to observe your surroundings. Look at a flower and ask yourself the following questions:

1. How is the petal shaped? (Make a simple sketch.)
2. How many petals are there? How are they arranged?
3. What overall pattern is formed as they radiate from the stem?
4. What shapes are formed by the repeated flowers?
5. What is the flower's general size in relation to the foliage?
6. What is the general shape of the leaves? (Make another sketch.)
7. How do the leaves extend from the stem?

These questions become the design elements in your quilt.

There is a difference if you are observing flowers in a landscape. The *Perennial Garden* quilt showcases flowers in a landscape. To plan this quilt, I used photographs of different gardens, noting pockets of color rather than individual flower shapes. Since I am a very textural person, I have more confidence when I use the fabric, rather than working with pencil and paper. I cut shapes and audition fabrics as I plan the design.

Don't be afraid to begin working even though you might not have all the answers. And don't let technical problems squash your creativity. Oftentimes I will visualize how something will look, but haven't yet figured out how to construct it. Trust yourself to solve the structural problems and get past the roadblocks along the way.

Try "possibility thinking." Make a list of possible solutions without being judgmental. In the process of looking for a solution, open your mind to ideas and you will find a solution. It is always easier to eliminate once your plate is full of possibilities. It may not happen immediately, but you have started the solution process and it will work. Trust me.

The creative process is well worth the rewards. Most people who make quilts give themselves challenges from time to time. I think one of the reasons that quiltmaking has evolved to the point that it has is that it nurtures creativity in people. Problem-solving is a normal part of the creative process, so I don't fight it. I just keep going. Seeing the process through to the end will allow you the experience of euphoria from completing a project. Euphoria is not something that every human being experiences, so enjoy it and give yourself a pat on the back.

garden patch

a garden plan— substitute simple vegetable shapes

Choosing Fabric

A Fabric Palette

Most of the fabrics in the quilts in this book have a floral or foliage mood. With these fabrics I look for movement in the print, similar to the look of a leaf, the petals of a flower, or the texture of a path. The fabrics that are the most difficult to find are what I call "transition" fabrics. They are the ones that you need when the leaves and sky come together and you don't want the straight line of the piecing to dominate. Often you just need a couple of pieces of a print to make the design work. I have even gone to some of my friends' homes to search for those little touches of fabric that I needed. (Of course, you find a fabric that is green and blue when you need a fabric that is yellow and green.) Or maybe you need a print that transitions from a flower shape to leaves. For the *Sunflowers* quilt, I used an actual sunflower in the print to help me with the overall design.

Pull any possible fabrics from your collection that might work in the composition. At this point you are gathering, so don't eliminate yet. Be very open-minded, be a possibility thinker! Just because you are making a floral quilt in pinks with foliage, don't overlook the foliage in another print. There may be a print with bright orange flowers that has great foliage.

I gather fabrics over a period of time before I actually begin working on a quilt. Giving yourself time to think about the impression you want to make may offer more possibilities when you start on the quilt. It is easier to find the "right" fabric over a period of time…you can check various stores, or ask friends at quilt group. Maybe a friend is willing to share a piece of perfect red fabric for those poppies in your meadow quilt. In the process of collecting, you will give yourself a good palette. Remember, you won't use everything. But it is always easier to eliminate than try to find that one last fabric that the design needs desperately. Use the following guidelines to help you with this selection process.

Contrast

Make sure you have contrast. Contrast is the relationship of light and dark beween colors. Lighter fabrics are needed to help define the darker shapes, and vice versa.

Is there an accent fabric? An accent is a small amount of a color that is definitely lighter, darker, or brighter than its surrounding colors that will make the composition "sing."

Have you created interest in each major color family? Are there several fabric shades within an area? An example is the *Perennial Garden* quilt. Look closely at the photograph and you will see a deep maroon color mixed in with the lighter pinks. The darker color helps define the area and give it interest.

Scale

Look for a variety in the scale of prints. Scale refers to the size of the elements in the design. Large floral designs will have areas that give texture and a particular color when needed. Medium scale fabrics are good for showcasing a particular flower or leaf. Look for low contrast prints that can work as "blenders." These fabrics add a sense of calmness to a design.

A variety in the scale of the prints adds interest and movement to the design. Individual templates can be cut from a large leaf print to create a swirl, or add motion or direction when placed within a design. Look closely at the fabrics used in the different quilts.

Style of Fabric

Keep the style of the fabric the same as the impression you are trying to make. For example, tiny "cutesy" designs in muted country colors are not the style of fabric that would usually work in an impressionistic floral quilt. Look at the texture that is created. Is there movement? Are there parts of a larger print that might work, even though the rest of the print doesn't? I use medium to larger scale prints with flowing lines to give the impression of flowers and foliage. When using a variety of prints, the fabrics need to be the same weight and texture because you'll be cutting and stitching together a lot of small pieces. (Fabrics don't have to be 100% cotton, but they are easier to use if they are.) Develop your "critical eye" to search for the perfect fabrics.

The Quilt Design

Using a traditional patchwork block or a grid, you can create an impression of a garden, bouquet, or mountain meadow full of wildflowers. Much like a painter works with brush strokes, you will work with bits and pieces of fabric in a palette to create a floral impression. Approach the design process as a painter challenges a working canvas. Always question, "What does the design need?" A problem area one day may lead to an opportunity the next. This style of quilt is formed by an ongoing process. Start with a photograph or picture that suggests a mood to you (or sketch colors and shapes as I did in the *Perennial Garden* quilt), and then determine the block or piecing technique that offers you the best opportunity to project the impression. As you look at the various quilts in the book you will see a variety of piecing styles. I begin by using traditional blocks with simple grids and then create interest in the fabric and color placement. You can add to this process, as I have done, by designing your own blocks, however simple or complicated they may be.

Look at the shapes that make up the composition. Note the individual shape of the flowers and foliage (refer to page 6 for ideas on observation). What traditional grid or block shapes might relate to these shapes? In *Sunflowers*, I saw the flowers with triangular shaped petals and circle centers. I saw the leaves as one shape, but in nature some flopped over to form wedge shapes. The blue fabric, suggesting the sky between the leaves, also formed wedges. In *Bachelor's Buttons*, the arcs of the New York Beauties mimic the spiky petals of the flowers. Setting the arc on point in a pieced Nine Patch block gave me the opportunity to create a bed of greenery. I thought of the bachelor's buttons in my garden. The blue sky filters through the leaves and flowers as I sit on the ground pulling the weeds around them. Also, an invaluable tool to use is a reducing glass. It allows you to observe the quilt from a distance and see how the shapes come together.

Be objective when you view a photo or picture. Study the picture and make notes in your journal. Ask yourself, "What are the proportions of the colors that I see?" If the picture is pleasing to you, follow the same color proportions and the quilt should be pleasing. Look at the individual areas of color. When you look at the greens, what kind of greens are they? Are they yellow-greens, deep dark greens, blue-greens, sage-greens, or a combination. Observing what colors make up the composition will help later when choosing fabrics.

Grid Design

Make a grid on paper or photocopy one from the book. Place a piece of tracing paper on top of the grid and secure the corners with masking tape. Using colored pencils, randomly sketch the color areas while referring to your inspirational photograph. This doesn't have to be exact; it is an impression. It gives you a working sketch with a grid base. Determine the approximate size of the quilt.

When I started designing *Bachelor's Buttons,* I thought the quilt would be more vertical. But as I progressed, the design didn't look right. I finally tried making the quilt more horizontal. This really helped. Although determining the parameters ahead of time gives you a field to work in, be open to changing the design size.

Cutting Instructions

To figure the yardage, I double the size of the quilt to account for the seaming and fabric that doesn't work. Then I use these proportions to obtain the yardage. Next, I cut portions from all of the fabrics that I think have a possibility of making it into the quilt. If a fabric is a large leaf design and I will only need 2" squares, I wait until I want one of the squares. In most of the quilts, the individual pieces were cut as I went along. (Cutting instructions are given in the chapters for each of the grids, and yardage requirements are based on 42" width.)

For the piecing, make the templates from template plastic. (The quilts are pieced together using a ¼" seam allowance unless otherwise noted.) Use a rotary cutter and ruler to cut around the template. Proceed very slowly and make sure your fingers are holding the middle of the template. You will find that the perfect spot on the fabric for the template is not always on grain. This is OK! There are enough fabrics that will be on grain to control these pieces, so don't be afraid to move the template around until you are satisfied with the design. This may leave holes in the fabric, but just use the rest of it in another project.

The Design Wall

You will have greater success in the design process if you tack a large piece of flannel on a wall to view your design as you work. Flannel is also available with a preprinted grid on it to help with placement of the fabric pieces. If you do not have a wall that will work, I suggest that you buy a piece of foam-core board and tack the flannel to the board. Pull the flannel edges to the backside of the board, and then pin or glue the edges. (Foam-core board is available at craft or hardware stores and framing shops.) Prop the board up against a wall while you work. When you are finished, pin tissue paper over the design and keep it under the bed or behind the sofa. If the piece gets too large, you will have to stitch it together once you are satisfied and start another section.

While you are working on the quilt, it is very useful to use a reducing glass to look at the pieces of fabric you have placed on the wall. During the design process everything looks great when you are standing right in front of the design, but when the project is viewed from a distance sometimes the colors are "too comfortable" together and become boring. A change may be needed to make the image more as you envisioned it. Use your "critical eye" to create the impression you want to make and remember to view the composition from a distance to determine whether it is working or not.

Creating the Quilt

While you work on your design, always keep the photograph or picture that inspired the design and the sketch you made next to the design board. Lay the fabric you have already cut out in color groups on a nearby table. Begin working an area of the quilt by placing the cut fabric on the flannel wall. Create interest in that section by using a variety of fabric styles even if you are using one color group. A larger print texture will balance out a smaller all-over pattern or a two-color print.

Think of the process as auditioning the fabrics for the quilt. Don't get hung up on having to use a particular fabric because it may not work. Use your "objective eye" while you work. If the fabric doesn't look good in that area, then it might work someplace else—or it may not work at all. If you follow this process you will find yourself becoming more objective and creative at the same time. Remember, Please the quilt! Ask yourself, "What does the quilt need?"

From time to time, stand back from the design and use the reducing glass to see how it is progressing. I like coming downstairs in the morning and seeing the quilt with fresh eyes. My creativity is the best in the morning, so I do my design work then. During other parts of the day I sew, since the decisions are already made. Determine your best design time and enjoy the rest of the time spent in creating your design. This is an ongoing process and will take time. It is similar to planting a garden, nurturing it, and watching it grow.

You might want to refer to the discussion on design in "The Creative Process" on page 6. I find that I sometimes need to remind myself that I am in a process and I do have the decision-making ability to get it done or solve the problem. I have to be patient when I hit a road block and so will you. Once you are happy with the design, then you can start stitching the pieces together. Instructions are given with each quilt on how to sew it together.

While I am creating the quilt, I constantly think about how I might want to finish the edges. Will it need a border? Is there an edge design shape that might work? How might I quilt it? At this time I try to think of ways to enhance the design. One way of doing that is to repeat or echo the design elements. This happened in the scalloped border on *Bachelor's Buttons*. In the quilt design, the curve of the flower shape is repeated around the edge of the quilt. Be on the look out for elements that will enhance the quilt: an accent border strip, a shape for a quilting design. Repetition in the design elements will give the quilt continuity and unify the elements.

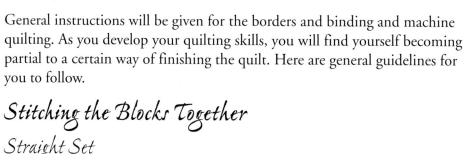

General instructions will be given for the borders and binding and machine quilting. As you develop your quilting skills, you will find yourself becoming partial to a certain way of finishing the quilt. Here are general guidelines for you to follow.

Stitching the Blocks Together

Straight Set

Always lay out the quilt blocks before you begin sewing so that you can be sure they are in a pleasing order. Stitch the blocks together in rows. Press seam allowances toward the right on odd-numbered rows and toward the left on even-numbered rows when applicable. Then join row 2 to row 1, row 3 to row 2, and so on. When you join the rows, the seam allowances that you pressed in opposite directions will automatically nest together.

Diagonal Set

In a diagonal set, the rows run across the quilt at a 45° angle (on point). Sew the blocks together in diagonal rows. Press the seam allowances in the opposite directions so that the seams will nest together when joining the rows. The corner triangles are added last.

Adding Borders

Borders can act as a frame for quilts. To attach a border strip, start at one side of the quilt. Lay the right side of the border strip on the right side of the quilt and pin the two layers together. With the back facing you, stitch ¼" from the edge, making sure the seam allowances are sewn down in the direction that you originally pressed them. Press both seam allowances toward the border. Repeat for the other side of the quilt. Add the top and bottom border strips using the same process as the sides.

Mitered Corners for Borders

This is a simple method that works for me. When cutting the border strips, leave an extra length that is the width of the border at the end of each strip. Example: leave an <u>extra</u> 2" at each end of a 2" wide border.

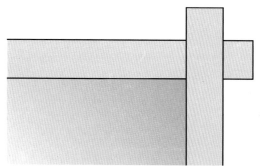

1 Stitch the borders to the quilt, stopping ¼" from each corner of the quilt. Back tack one or two stitches. This leaves the seam allowance free at the corner. Press the seam allowances toward the border.

2 For the next few steps, work at the ironing board. At this point the two borders at the corner are overlapping.

Working from the right-hand side, turn the seam allowance under to form a 45° diagonal line from the corner to the outside edge. Press the fold.

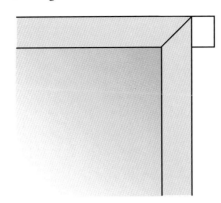

Gently lift up the border at the right and put pins at the fold through both fabrics.

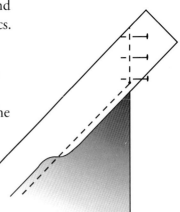

3 Stitch from the corner of the quilt to the outside edge. The seam allowances will be free. Back tack at each end. Trim the excess fabric and press the seam open.

Quilting

For most of these quilts, the intricate piecing and variety of fabrics made the design complete in itself. I chose to machine quilt in the ditch to secure the layers. It would be very difficult to hand quilt through all of the seams in these quilts. How much quilting should be done is a personal decision, but be sure there is enough quilting to hold the layers in place. For the bachelor's buttons' stems, like lines were quilted. Sometimes repetitive lines were stitched from the flower shape to emphasize the shape. On the border of *Perennial Garden* the floral shapes in the print were outlined.

Cotton batting works best in wall quilts. I find that the polyester battings with loft sometimes create ripples along the sides of quilts, so I like the flatter battings or just flannel when I have used a foundation fabric in the piecing. Be sure to baste often before beginning. I baste with safety pins when I am going to machine quilt.

Binding

Cut the binding strips 1¾" wide and on the straight of grain. One exception is the *Bachelor's Buttons* quilt; it needed bias binding because of the scallops.

1 Stitch the side bindings to the front of the quilt, with right sides together. I like to use the same walking foot for binding that I use for quilting. It keeps the edge from creeping. Trim off any excess fabric. Turn under the raw edge ¼" and press.

2 Slipstitch the pressed edge to the back of the quilt. Add the top and bottom binding, leaving ½" at each end to turn under. Finish the corners as shown. This makes a nice square corner.

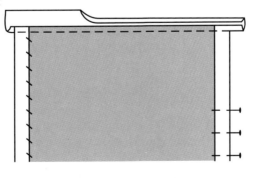

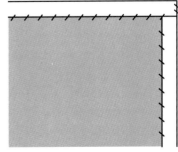

tuck under seam allowances and stitch

Chapter 2

Cottage Garden

by Valori Wells

Simple House blocks have always been a favorite of mine. Look closely at the houses in this quilt and you will see a variety of floral prints and styles in a wide range of colors. As I create a scrap quilt, I plan some form of repetition in the quilt for design continuity: all of the houses are floral fabrics and the roof is a contrasting fabric of a dense print fabric. The arrangement of the scrap fabrics works well because the blocks are consistent, and they are also surrounded by sky-blue fabric sashing. The buttonhole stitching adds a special decorative touch. This quilt is a good project for experimenting with floral fabrics, or if you're expanding into more contemporary quiltmaking.

Materials

- Background fabric for House blocks: 1 yard
- Scrap fabrics for houses, roofs, and chimneys: 1 yard total, or approximately a 9" square for each house
- Sashing, Border, and Binding: 1 yard
- Six-strand embroidery floss for buttonhole stitching: 2 skeins total of complementary colors
- Paper-backed (sewable) adhesive (16" wide): 1⅛ yards
- Backing: 1¼ yards

The finished size is 40" x 40". The finished block size is 8".

Instructions

1 Cut sixteen 8½" squares from the background fabric. Set aside. Trace one house, roof, and two chimney patterns onto the paper side of the adhesive. To streamline cutting the patterns, cut three more squares of adhesive and layer the squares with the paper side up. Then place the traced patterns on top of the stack. Pin in three places to secure the layers. Cut around the patterns. Repeat the process three more times for a total of 16 houses.

2 Work one block at a time. Place the adhesive (paper side up) onto the wrong side of the appliqué fabrics. Following the manufacturer's instructions, fuse the adhesive to the fabric. Cut out the shapes. Peel off the paper backing. Position the appliqué shapes onto the background blocks, leaving an ample ¼" around the block edges for the seam allowance. Leave a space between the shapes for the decorative stitching. Fuse the houses in place following the manufacturer's instructions.

3 Using two strands of embroidery floss, buttonhole stitch around all the appliqué shapes. To start, cut an 18" length of floss. Separate two strands from the cut floss, place the two strands together and knot one end. Bring the threaded needle up from the back of the fabric to appear at the raw

edge of the appliqué shape, and pull the thread through to the knot. Approximately ⅛" to ¼" from the raw edge, insert the needle into the shape and emerge parallel to the raw edge, bringing the needle tip over the working thread. Pull the stitch into place until the thread along the edge is secure and slightly taut. Hold the working thread with your left thumb and take another stitch. Repeat the process to continue stitching.

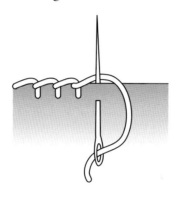

When you reach a corner, stitch over the working thread, but then insert the needle into the fabric to form a small catch stitch. This ends the stitch. Bring the needle up again (at the dot) a couple of threads away and continue stitching.

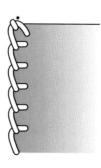

4 For the sashing and borders, cut ten 2" x 42" strips. From these strips, cut twelve 8½" lengths for the vertical sashing between the blocks. Cut five 37" strips for the horizontal sashing and side borders. Cut two 40" strips for the top and bottom borders.

5 Assemble the blocks and vertical sashing together into horizontal rows. Press the seams toward the sashing. Join the horizontal rows and sashing together: row 1 to sashing to row 2, etc. Add the side borders, and then the top and bottom borders to the quilt. Press the seams toward the borders.

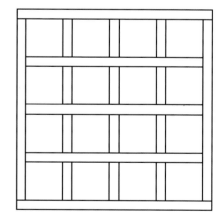

6 Finish the quilt following the instructions on page 14. The quilt was quilted by stitching in the ditch between the blocks and around the houses. The sashing was quilted by stitching diagonally to form a crosshatch design.

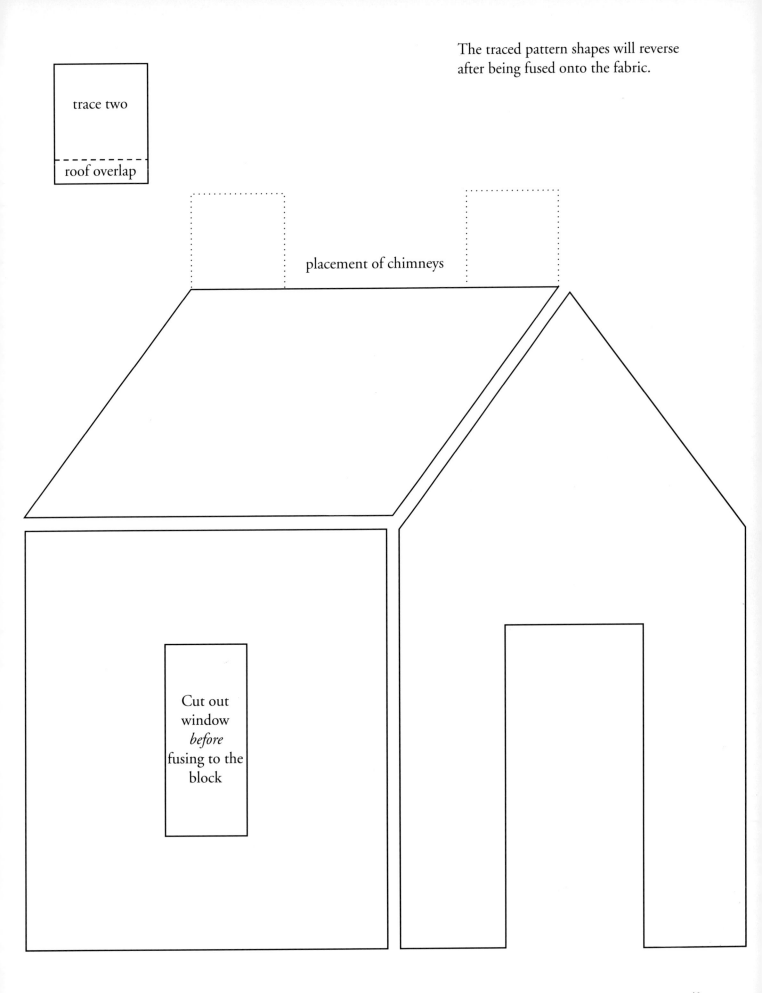

trace two

roof overlap

The traced pattern shapes will reverse after being fused onto the fabric.

placement of chimneys

Cut out window *before* fusing to the block

Pressed Flowers

Pressing flowers is exciting! Let it become a special way for you to capture the beauty of your garden. Pressed flowers are lasting reminders to you and those you share them with of the beauty of mother nature. I still have pressed flowers from my grandmother that I use in my projects. Sometimes they do fade, but this often gives the flowers more character.

I have found that some of the best flowers to press are wildflowers. They are very tiny and delicate. If the flower is too thick, such as a Shasta daisy, it has too much moisture to just simply press it. (Fortunately, flowers that are too thick can be preserved in other ways: their petals and leaves can be pressed individually.) The following flowers are easy to press: Queen Anne's lace, English daisies, gypsophila, jasmine, asters (the smaller, more delicate ones), forget-me-nots, Johnny-jump-ups, violas, and pansies. The best thing to do is experiment—you never know what will work. Sometimes the back sides of petals and leaves have intricate designs and are more attractive than the fronts when used in your creations.

Leaves and herbs are also wonderful to press, and greenery adds a lot to a collage of pressed flowers. For greenery you can use mint leaves, chamomile, lavender leaves, ferns, ivy leaves and stems, parsley, sage, clover, thyme, and the leaves from your flowers.

The best time to cut flowers is in the morning, just after the dew has evaporated. For me, this isn't always possible, so I cut them before it gets too hot (and they begin to wilt) or in the evening (when it is cool but the flowers have not closed). As long as a flower isn't wilted or wet, it can be pressed.

There are two ways I have found that are good for pressing flowers: First, old phone books work great. Insert the flowers into the pages, then put several heavy books on top of a flower-filled phone book to ensure thorough pressing. The second method is to use a flower press. A flower press is easy to make and doesn't cost much. All you need is two 12" square pieces of plywood, 4½" bolts (all thread bolts are the best), four wing nuts, eight to ten pieces of 10" square cardboard (sometimes corrugated cardboard will leave lines in the flowers, but it helps keep air circulating through the press while the flowers are drying), sixteen to eighteen pieces of 10" square blotter paper, and a drill. Drill a hole in each corner of the plywood, about ¾" from the edge. I suggest when you put the bolts into the bottom piece of the press that you glue them down. (I've found that when you are tightening down the wing nut sometimes the bolts will just rotate and nothing is accomplished.) Remember to glue the bottom side, and not the side that the blotter paper is going to be on. If you decide to glue the bolts, let the glue sit overnight before adding the wing nuts. Cut the corners off the cardboard and the blotter paper, but cut just enough so the edges do not touch the bolts.

Assemble the flower press so that there are two pieces of blotter paper between each piece of cardboard. Lay the flowers between the two pieces of blotter paper making sure they don't touch each other, or they will be difficult to get apart when they are dry. Then lay the piece of cardboard on top. Keep adding

layers until you run out of flowers or blotter paper, and then carefully place the other piece of plywood on top. Gently tighten down the wing nuts. Tighten each corner as evenly as possible so as not to disturb the position of the flowers. Tighten just enough so that the cardboard is flat.

Let the flowers dry. (It usually takes a week or two.) The flowers should be completely dry before you remove them from the press. If they feel damp or don't slide off the blotter paper easily, put the top back on and tighten the wing nuts again.

Garden Fences

by Diane Rupp

The idea for this quilt came at just the right time. My husband and I had moved during the middle of winter and I needed cheering up. The fabrics did the trick—they were sunny, floral, and colorful—I loved them all. I had never worked with so many of my favorite fabrics in one quilt. The only difficult part was having to choose which strip of fabric to use next. The inspiration for the courthouse step piecing came from an antique Log Cabin quilt that Jean Wells had just purchased.

Medium to smaller floral designs work best in this quilt. If you keep in mind the ½"-wide finished log size, it's easy to see why. Large florals either have too much background or come across as solids. Also, unlike the blending techniques in watercolor style quilts, I found the logs needed to contrast with one another. To create contrast and add interest, I sporadically placed unlike fabrics next to each other and added spots of intense color throughout. Because I love pink and yellow together in a garden, I added extra pink to highlight the lighter floral fabrics. The soft colors contrast with the darker floral backgrounds. In addition, I used a kitten print fabric and little kittens are hidden in the design. Can you find them?

Materials

Garden Fences is truly a scrap quilt. Over 75 fabrics were used to compose the Log Cabin blocks. Each center square is yellow, with a courthouse steps arrangement of dark and light floral strips surrounding the center squares. Note the separate block configurations (on page 24) when selecting the fabrics.

- Center squares: ½ yard
- Dark floral scrap fabrics: 2¼ yards total
- Light floral scrap fabrics: 2 yards total
- Binding and Backing: 3⅞ yards

The finished size is 58¼" x 75". The finished block size is 5¼".

Instructions

1 There are three block configurations that make up the quilt. All of the blocks start with a yellow center square.

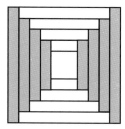

Center block

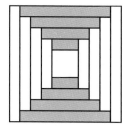

Border block

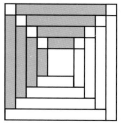

Corner block

2 For the center of the blocks, cut seven 1¾" x 42" strips from the yellow fabric. Cut the strips into thirty-nine 7" lengths. Cut a 1" x 42" strip each from the dark and light floral fabrics. You can cut more strips as you need them.

3 Make four Center blocks at a time. When the blocks are scattered throughout the design, the quilt will still look like a scrap quilt. Begin by stitching different light floral strips to the long sides of the 7" strips. (Trim off the extra floral strip lengths as you

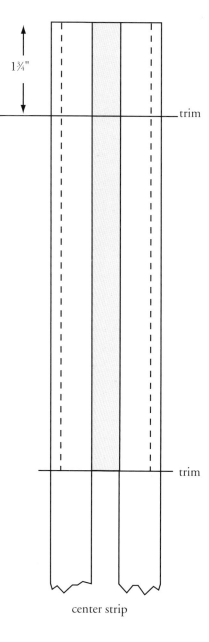

1¾"

trim

trim

center strip

work.) Press the seams toward the floral log pieces. Cut the pieced strips at 1¾" intervals.

4 Stitch a dark floral strip to the long sides of the cut units. Repeat the process, adding a set of light and dark floral strips to opposite sides of the unit, until four sets of logs have been added. Press the seams toward the log pieces. You will need 108 Center blocks for the body of the quilt.

5 Using the Border block illustration as a guide, repeat Steps 3-4. This time begin with the dark floral strips to construct forty-two Border blocks.

6 For the Corner blocks, you will need to pre-cut strips for one side only. These pre-cut strips are pieced together before the log strips are added to the block. Follow the illustration below to cut and piece the strips.

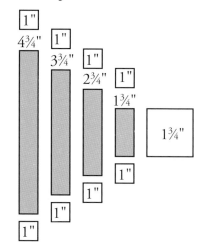

Using the Corner block illustration as a guide, add strips to center square in a counter clockwise Log Cabin manner to construct four Corner blocks. All four corner blocks are the same.

7 Arrange Center blocks in twelve horizontal rows with nine blocks in each row. Stitch the blocks together to form horizontal rows: join row 1 to row 2, etc. Press.

8 Stitch two sets of twelve Border blocks together for the side borders. Add the side borders to the quilt. Refer to the quilt photo for color arrangement. Press.

9 The long dark strips on the sides of the Center blocks form a natural border for the side of the quilt. To equal the border emphasis at the top and bottom of the quilt, nine different 1" x 5¾" dark floral strips are pieced together, and then a 1" square of light floral fabric is pieced to each end of the strip. A 1" x 4¾" dark

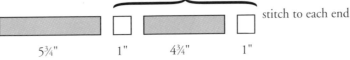

5¾"   1"   4¾"   1"   stitch to each end

floral strips is pieced to each end of the strip, and then another 1" square of light floral fabric is pieced to each end to complete the strip.

Assemble two pieced strips in this manner, and add to the top and bottom of the quilt. Press.

LOWER RIGHT CORNER

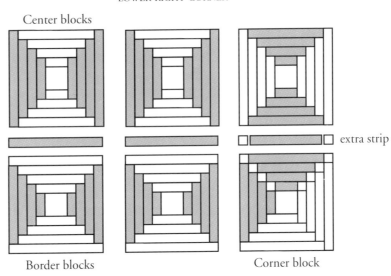

Center blocks

extra strip

Border blocks

Corner block

10 Stitch two sets of nine Border blocks together to form the top and bottom borders. Add a Corner block to each end of the top and bottom borders. Press. Add the top and bottom borders to the quilt. Refer to the quilt photo for placement.

11 Finish the quilt following the instructions on page 14. The quilt was machine quilted by stitching in the ditch between each block and in the middle of each log.

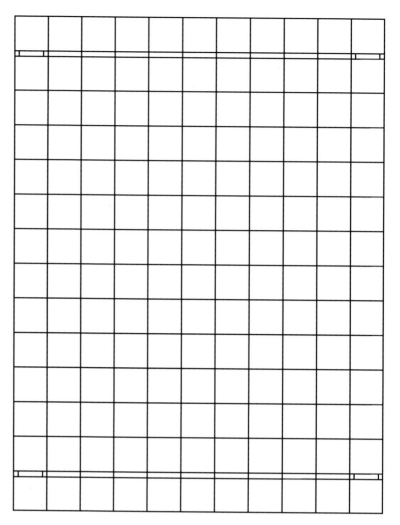

Language of Flowers

For centuries, the language of flowers has been used to express specific emotions, feelings, or thoughts to one another. I have found the meaning of specific flowers and the history behind the meaning very interesting. And although lavender means distrust, I still enjoy receiving a bundle of it. I thought you might enjoy knowing the meaning of some of your flowers. Sometimes books vary on the meaning, so you might know different meanings of the flowers listed.

Anemone: forsaken

Bachelor's button: celibacy

Bluebell: constancy

Buttercup: childhood

Chamomile: energy in adversity

Carnation, pink: woman's love

Chrysanthemum: cheerfulness

Columbine: resolution

Crocus: abuse not

Daffodil: regards

Daisy: innocence

Forget-me-not: true love

Foxglove: insincerity

French Marigold: jealousy

Gardenia: peace

Geranium, pink: partiality

Hibiscus: delicate beauty

Hollyhock: female ambition

Honeysuckle: rustic beauty

Hydrangea: boastfulness

Iris: I have a message for you

Ivy: friendship

Jasmine, yellow: grace & elegance

Larkspur: brightness

Lavender: distrust

Lilac: purity, modesty

Lily-of-the-valley: return of happiness

Magnolia: love of nature

Mint: virtue

Myrtle: love

Narcissus: self-interest, egotism

Pansy: thinking of you

Peony: anger

Peppermint: cordiality

Phlox: agreement

Poppy, red: consolation

Rhododendron: danger

Rambler Rose: only deserve my love

Rose, white: I am worthy of you

Rose, yellow: departure of love

Rosebud, red: you are young and beautiful

Rosebud, white: a heart ignorant of love

Sage: domestic virtue

Snapdragon: presumption

Sunflower: haughtiness

Tulip, red: declaration of love

Tulip, yellow: hopeless love

Verbena: enchantment

Violet, blue: faithfulness

Violet, white: modesty

Water Lily: purity of heart

Wisteria: regret

Yarrow: solace

Zinnia: thoughts of friends

Lady of the Garden I

Lady of the Garden

by Marrell Dickson

This scrap quilt has a floral garden theme. For me, designing with floral fabrics is a very elusive concept. Most of the time I feel that selecting complementary fabrics is an instinctive response. I have to tell myself, "Please the quilt." But in order to make the floral prints work together, I first had to realize green was a neutral color. This is how I now audition fabrics before I start to piece my quilt. I view the floral fabrics to see how they interplay with the greens. It gives me a feeling of what is going to happen in my quilt and at the same time lets me in on a few unexpected surprises—always positive! Greens are my earth tones. I prefer to use a nongeometric and monochromatic floral or leafy green print. A good exercise is to cut 2⅞" squares of as many greens—yellow-greens, gray-greens, blue-greens—as you can beg, borrow, or pinch, and note how they interact with each other.

Planning for traditional block quilts is a matter of finding the right pattern, and then planning the fabrics. For the summer version, different tone-on-tone greens in light to medium shades were used for the background. The fabrics have strong contrast and purity. In the spring version the green is all the same green fabric and the florals are softer. Look closely at the photo to see the repetitive placement of the prints. In the first block, the center square (A) is divided diagonally into two pieces. I used a large floral and a medium floral print for each piece. The half-square triangles (B) consist of small to medium floral prints with a green background print. By always repeating the placement, the quilt has continuity, even though it is a scrap quilt.

Materials

- Piece A: Assorted floral fabrics to total 1⅞ yards
- Piece B: Assorted floral fabrics to total 1¾ yards
- Pieces B, C: Assorted shades of light to medium green to total 2 yards
- Backing: 3⅓ yards
- Binding: ½ yard
- Optional: 2" grid paper for making half-square triangles

The finished size is 57" x 71". The finished block size is 10".

Instructions

Instructions are given for one block since no two are alike. When you cut a square for A and cut it diagonally, you will have two A's. One for this block and one for another.

1 For the center A block, cut a 6⅞" square from two different prints. Cut diagonally. You will use half of each. Put the two leftovers aside to use in another block.

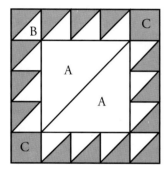

2 Use either Method I or Method 2 to construct the half-square triangles (B).

Method 1. This is the method I use to make my half-square triangles. Cut a 9" square from both green background and floral fabrics. Place the squares right sides together and press. Place seven squares of half-square 2" grid paper (the half-square triangles are printed on the paper) on top of the layers and pin together. There will be excess fabric around the edges. Following the manufacturer's instructions, stitch through the paper as indicated. Cut the pieces apart. Carefully remove the paper. Press the seams toward the green fabrics.

Method 2. Cut a 2⅞" x 22" strip from both green background and floral fabrics. Place the strips right sides together and press. Cut the strips into seven 2⅞" squares, and then cut the squares in half diagonally. Stitch together along the diagonal edge. Press the seams toward the green fabrics.

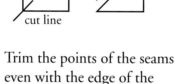

2⅞"

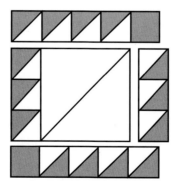

cut line

Trim the points of the seams even with the edge of the square.

3 Cut two 2½" squares for C from the green fabric.

4 Stitch the blocks together following the illustration. Press the seams toward the block center. Make 31 blocks.

For the filler blocks at the quilt edges, cut a 6⅞" square from a floral fabric, and then cut diagonally for A. Use either Method I or Method 2

(Step 2) to construct the half-square triangles (B). For Method I, cut a 6" square of both green background and floral fabrics. For Method 2, cut a 2⅞" x 12" strip of both green background and floral fabrics. Cut one 2⅞" square for C from the green background fabric, and then cut diagonally. Using the illustration as a guide, make 18 filler blocks.

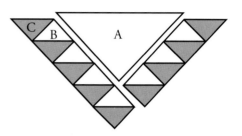

6 Using the photo as a guide, arrange the blocks for the quilt. All the blocks are placed on point, but in the horizontal rows of four blocks, the blocks are positioned so the seam in A is horizontal. In the rows of three blocks, the blocks are positioned so the seam is vertical.

Lady of the Garden II

7 Stitch the blocks together in diagonal rows. Press. Then join row 1 to row 2, etc. Press. The edges around the quilt are all bias seams so be careful not to stretch them while you sew.

8 Finish the quilt following the instructions on page 14. This quilt was quilted by stitching in the ditch between the blocks, between A and B, and at the center seam of A.

Cutting Flowers

The early morning or evening hours before the flowers have gone to bed are the best time for cutting flowers. Use a sharp knife or scissors to cut diagonally just above a node (where a leaf or stem grows from the stock). This type of cut will allow the plants to grow new flowers.

Remove the foliage three-fourths from the bottom of the stem. Place the cut flowers in a container of tepid water, keeping the blossoms dry. Take the container inside and cut the stems again at an angle, but keeping them underwater while you cut. This cut prevents blockage of water intake. Keep the flowers cool until you are ready to arrange them.

Flowers with woody stems that ooze sap need extra preparation. Poppies and dahlias are two of the flowers that exude a sticky fluid that can clog the stems. To prevent this, sear the stems with a flame for a few seconds. Some flowers with woody stems, such as lilacs, need to have the stems hammered slightly so the fibers break down and they can absorb water. There are also commercial preparations available at garden shops and hardware stores that make the flowers last longer. Add a few drops of this fluid to the water, and be sure to change the water every couple days.

Chapter 3

Perennial Garden

by Jean Wells

English perennial cottage garden scenes have always fascinated me. Using several ideas from numerous pictures, I sketched a design to create the *Perennial Garden* quilt. Looking at my sketch, I could see I needed a variety of prints positioned at different angles within each square to obtain an impressionistic effect. I chose a 1½" square grid with the squares set on point. I divided the squares into two half-square triangles. The half-square triangles could be set either vertically or horizontally, if needed. Once the grid was established, I started collecting fabrics for the quilt.

Using plastic templates, I cut several pieces of fabric in each color group for the cottage, path, foliage, and flowers. (This quilt needed a lot of individually cut pieces.) Working on my design wall, I used a variety of off-white fabric pieces to create the cottage. Then I added an off-white print with fine green vines to the corners of the cottage so the vines looked like they were growing up the side. For the roof a brown grass print was used that resembled a thatched roof once the pieces were together. Complementary floral prints create the windows and chimney. Once the cottage was assembled, the path was next.

My first path was all gray fabrics, but I took the quilt to my Flower Impressions class and everyone started to tell me that paths are also brown. Of course, I realized that what I needed was a transition fabric to go between the path and the flowers! The search was on for fabrics with a little brown or gray and pink or blue to transition between the flowers and path. Marrell Dickson, a quilting friend who is famous for her floral fabric collection, came to my rescue, and I found the perfect fabrics. From there I worked on the tree foliage behind and beside the cottage to create the skyline for the top of the quilt.

The remainder of the quilt was an experience similar to planting a garden. One day I worked in one flower bed, then the next day in another flower bed until the quilt was finished. I cut a lot of the pieces individually because I wanted each piece to work in the composition. My husband came down one day and commented on how my "puzzle" was coming along—it did look like a jigsaw puzzle as it progressed.

Jackie Erickson sews with me once a week. Her visits are like having the good fairy show up at the door. For this quilt, we set the sewing machine beside the design wall, with the iron nearby. Jackie started stitching the blocks together in diagonal rows; she joined one row to the next. It took a while to determine whether the quilt needed a border or not. I took it back to quilt class and got several opinions. In the end, the neutral floral print seemed to look the best with the design. It complemented both the path and the house, and gave dimension to the garden colors in the quilt. The folded strip of dark green fabric inset between the quilt and second border added a pleasing touch to the design.

Materials

You will need a variety of prints to total 2½ yards for piecing. The sky comprises approximately 14% of the design, the foliage 31%, the path 12%, the cottage 22%, and the flowers 21%. Use the photograph as a guide when selecting your fabrics.

- First Border Inset: ⅛ yard
- Second Border and Binding: ⅔ yard
- Backing 1¼ yards

The finished size is 37" x 45½". The finished block size is 1½" square.

Instructions

1 Use the patterns of the square and half-square triangle to create a set of templates. The ¼" seam allowances are already included in the patterns.

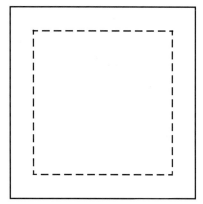

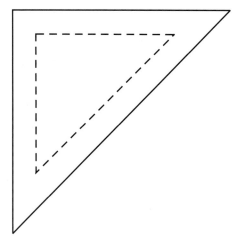

2 Identify the area of the quilt where you want to begin working. Cut several squares and half-square triangles. Then as you see what the quilt needs, cut individual pieces to complete the design. You will find that there are many areas to add transition fabrics: the sky and trees, the path and flowers, or from one group of flowers to foliage areas. You may find yourself going to your fabric collection to look for just the right fabric. Keep in mind as you work the design that the

half-square triangles can be placed either horizontally or vertically in the design.

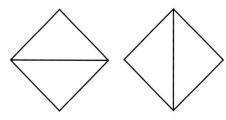

3 Once you are happy with the design, stitch the half-square triangles together into squares. Press. Trim the points of the seam even with the edge of the square. Then stitch the squares into rows diagonally. Stitch the diagonal rows together: join row 1 to row 2, etc. If you stitch from the top down on the first row, stitch from the bottom up on the next row to prevent the quilt from stretching in one direction. Press the seams in one direction.

4 With a straight ruler, carefully trim off the extra fabric at the edges of the quilt, keeping a ¼" seam allowance.

5 For the first border, cut two 1" x 40⅞" strips for the top and bottom and two 1" x 32⅜" strips for the sides. Fold the fabric in half lengthwise with wrong sides together, and press. Pin the top and bottom borders to the quilt, carefully matching the edges. You may need to ease in some fullness to the edges. This border will actually help to square up the quilt. Stitch the border strip to the quilt ³⁄₁₆" from the raw edges. Add the side strips, overlapping the strips at the corners.

6 For the second border, cut four 2¾" x 42" strips and one 2¾" x 20" strip. Trim two of the strips to 40⅞" for the sides. Stitch the remaining strips together into one long length, and trim two strips to 49⅜" for the top and bottom.

7 Since the second border will be mitered at the corners, place a pin 4½" from the end of each strip. Then place another pin ¼" from the edge of the quilt at each corner. With right sides facing, match the pin on the border strip to the pin on the quilt edge. Sew the border strips to the quilt from pin to pin. The remaining 4½" at the end of each strip will be used for mitering. Press the seams toward the border.

8 Miter one corner at a time, referring to the instructions on page 14.

9 Finish the quilt following the instructions on page 14. This quilt was machine quilted by stitching in the ditch on the diagonal seam lines, and free-form stitching around the floral designs in the border print.

(See page 2 for photocopy permission of pages 38 and 39.)

Seed Packet

Color photocopy the flower packet. Cut around the edges and fold along the lines.
Glue together leaving the top open. Fill it with seeds from your garden.
Decorate with pressed flowers if you like.

Wildflowers

by Valori Wells

Flowers have been an inspiration to me since I was a little girl. My mother always had a garden, and I grew up with flowers in the yard, flowers set in vases year round, and floral colors throughout our home. Now I am a photography major in college, but it is easy to guess my favorite subject matter.

I am amazed at the delicate shapes and variety of colors of the wildflowers. Larkspurs in purples and poppies in red and orange, yellow cone flowers, Indian paintbrush, and multicolored bachelor's buttons and lupine appear against a meadow of green grass. I like how nature integrates green within a rainbow of colors.

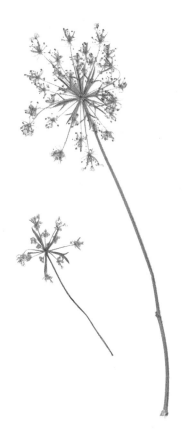

For this quilt, I portrayed a field of wildflowers. I wanted the quilt to have a playful look, as well as delicate charm. The pyramid block pattern worked for the style of fabric I chose. I sketched the design using colored pencils and pyramid graph paper. After observing the photographs I had taken of meadows, I determined the grouping of colors for the flowers. All of the colors are from my mom's collection of hand-dyed fabrics. I wanted a variety of colors, but they needed to have the same mood, or color coherency. Using the graduated shades of the flower colors available, it was possible to use different shades together, making the design more interesting.

I cut all of the shapes using a template and rotary cutter. The first border of the quilt is a folded inset strip of coral fabric. A batik fabric forms the second border. If you look closely, you will see where two different colorations of the same print fabric are pieced at an angle. (I wanted this to be a subtle change.)

Materials

You will need a variety of prints to total 2¾ yards for piecing. The blue of the sky comprises approximately 25% of the design, the ground and foliage 50%, and the flowers 25%.

- First Border Inset: ¼ yard
- Second Border and Binding: One or two fabrics to total ⅞ yard
- Backing: 2⅞ yards

The finished size is 46½" x 57".

Instructions

1 Use the pyramid pattern provided to make a plastic template to cut the fabric pieces. If you choose to work with hand-dyed fabrics, I recommend cutting only a few pieces at a time to avoid waste. Cut the assorted fabric pieces to form the design. Create the sky and ground first, and then start filling in the meadow with flowers and grass.

2 Set the size parameters on the design wall, sixteen across and sixteen down. Once the pieces are in place, stitch the pyramid blocks together into horizontal rows, and press. Stitch the rows together: join row 1 to row 2, etc. Press.

trim   trim

3 For the first border, cut five 1" x 42" strips of fabric. Join three strips together into one long strip, and trim two strips to 50½" for the side borders. Cut the remaining two strips to 39⅞" for the top and bottom borders. Fold the fabric in half lengthwise with wrong sides together, and press. Pin the top and bottom borders to the quilt, carefully matching the edges. You may need to ease in some fullness.

This border will actually help to square up the quilt. Stitch the border strips to the quilt ³⁄₁₆" from the raw edges. Add the side strips, overlapping them at the corners.

4 For the second border, cut five 3¾" x 42" strips. If you wish to use two fabrics, as I have done, piece the strips together before you add them to the quilt. Stitch three strips together into one long strip, then cut two 3¾" x 57" strips for the side borders. Cut two

3¾" x 39⅞" strips for the top and bottom borders.

5 Add the second border strips. Press the seams toward the border strips.

6 Finish the quilt following the instructions on page 14. This quilt was machine quilted by stitching in the ditch on the diagonal seam lines. The quilted grid design is repeated in the border.

Journal or Scrapbook

1 Use a purchased book, or make a book of your own. To make your own book, purchase plain paper for the inside sheets, and a thicker or heavier paper for the cover and the back. I used handmade paper for the book cover and back.

2 Bind the book before decorating the cover, or you could damage the flowers. Using the illustration as a guide, mark the holes at the edge of the front and back covers with a pencil.

3 Assemble the paper sheets inside the covers. Stack the layers as evenly as possible—if it is a bigger book, you can always add weight (another book) to stabilize the area that is not going to have holes punched in it.

4 Carefully poke the holes into the book with an ice pick, or other sharp tool. Don't try to get the ice pick all the way through the last page, but get at least an indentation of the point of the pick. Then you can lift up the book and poke out the rest of the back page, or pages, so the holes are the same size as the front pages.

5 Thread an embroidery needle with approximately a 24" length of silk ribbon. Lay three twigs down on the front cover (if needed, use a little glue to secure them while you are binding the book). Make sure the twigs are placed between the holes.

6 Using the threaded ribbon, randomly stitch the book together going over and under the twigs as you work. I threaded the book

together by judging how it looked: there was no pattern. Tie off the ends either inside the back cover or in a bow on the front cover.

7 Decorate the cover as you choose, following the instructions for the Pressed Flower Collages on page 64.

Daisies

by Jean and Valori Wells

Since I was a little girl, daisies have been one of my favorite flowers. Daisies are very easy to grow in our mountain climate because of our cold winters and short, hot summers. For this quilt, I wanted to capture the fresh look of the white and yellow flower with the deep green leaves; it is the same theme I used for my wedding many years ago. I designed this as a symmetrical quilt with the deep dark greens on the perimeter of the quilt forming the look of a pieced border. As the eye travels to the center of the quilt, transitions form: the greens get lighter and yellows are apparent within the prints. Then, the whites start appearing almost as if you were looking at the flowers close up. A variety of prints add texture to the white. Bright yellow triangles appear in speckles, looking like the centers of the flowers themselves. The impression is of a field of daisies with the intense contrast of the white and green with yellow speckles here and there.

The Hour Glass block was chosen because of the quarter-square triangle shape. This repeated shape gave me the opportunity to move colors around without having the blocks look repetitious. I wanted the placement of the yellow to look random in the quilt design.

Materials

You will need a variety of prints to total 2¾ yards for piecing. The yardage is based on strip cutting the triangles. The green comprises approximately 60% of the design, white 30%, and yellow 10%.

- Binding: ¼ yard
- Backing: 1¾ yards

The finished size is 44½" x 44½". The finished block size is 4" square.

Instructions

1 Use the pattern provided to make a plastic template. Cut the fabric pieces. The ¼" seam allowance is included in the pattern.

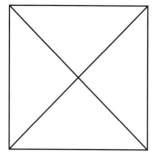

cut diagonally from corner to corner

If you don't mind cutting extra pieces that might not make it into the quilt, you can layer the fabric six deep. Cut 5¼" x 21" strips. From these strips, cut into four 5¼" squares. Cut the squares twice in half diagonally. You will still need to cut a few pieces for special placement in the design.

2 Begin designing the quilt by placing eleven different dark green triangles along the top edge. Then work down each side with eleven pieces and then continue across the bottom edge. You have now set the size parameters of the quilt.

3 Start working by referring to the color placement in the photo. Take time to look at what you are doing from a distance. Make adjustments.

4 When you are satisfied with the effect, stitch the pieces of the block together: Stitch two triangles of each block together along one short edge. Repeat with the remaining two triangles. Press the seams in opposite directions. Stitch the quarter-square triangles together along the long edge to complete the blocks. Press the seam in one direction. Trim the points of the seam even with the block.

5 Stitch the blocks into horizontal rows, and press. Stitch the rows together: join row 1 to row 2, etc.

6 Finish the quilt following the instructions on page 14. This quilt was machine quilted by stitching in the ditch on all the major seam lines.

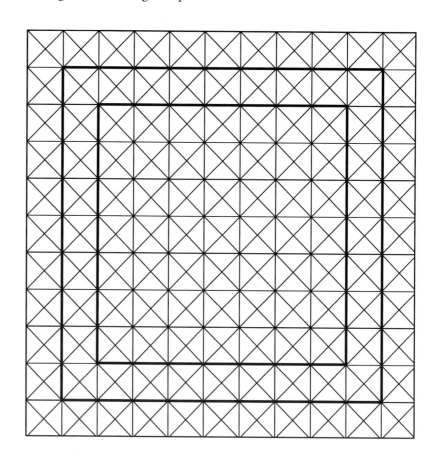

Flower Arranging

Flower arranging can be as simple as cutting flowers from the garden, arranging them in your hand, and then inserting them in a jelly jar. Over the years I have collected various small containers. As you can tell from the photo, three small vases of tiny fragile flowers are very effective as an arrangement.

Look in your cupboards for different containers. Water pitchers, glasses, stemware, jars, and bowls will all work for flower display. Clean the containers before you add the arrangement. If there is residue left over from previous flowers, wash the vase thoroughly with soap and water and a little ammonia, then rinse and dry the container.

For casual arrangements, fill a container three-fourths with water. Cut the stems of the main flowers all the same length. Because my garden is mostly perennials and wildflowers, some of the flower stems are very short or the flowers are tiny and fragile. These flowers should extend above the container at least one third so don't cut the stems too short. Put one cut flower in the container, then add another flower opposite the first. Continue until you have at least seven to eight main flower stems. Then start to fill in with some foliage or a second type of flower.

Casual, informal flower arrangements are less intimidating. I use foliage from my herb garden or other plants that grow in the yard. Sometimes three or four roses is all that you need. With wildflowers, I find that some of their stems are so fragile that it only takes three or four stems in a small vase to make a statement. They are simple and wispy.

When it comes to the color of the arrangement, anything goes. Think about how nature deals with color when you create your nosegay. There are many different greens as background colors and all flower colors mix and match beautifully.

O'Donnell's Irish Roses

by Virginia Busby O'Donnell

As a former math teacher, and a lover of geometry, the fact that there is a pattern to be made is a great part of the excitement I feel in making a quilted piece. For this particular quilt, I used hexagon-grid paper and colored in the sketch with pencils to get the design I wanted. The size of the hexagon determines the size of the quilt. If you want larger hexagons, just enlarge the pattern. By dividing some of the hexagons into three diamonds, I could get a three-dimensional look for the roses, which also increased the number of pieces to 2,421. This English paper-piecing project was the hand project I carried with me from 1992 to 1993 to keep me from becoming bored as I traveled, or kept me patient as I waited for appointments.

Hoffman Fabrics happened to be printing a fantastic green fabric and reddish-pink print that I could selectively cut pieces to get the contrast in colors for the quilt. I had plans to enter this piece in a contest and really had to push myself to finish in time— only to discover that I was no longer eligible for the contest. But at my house this quilt is a winner!

Materials

You will need a variety of prints to total 2 yards for piecing. The greens comprise approximately 67% of the design and the pinks 33%.

- Backing and Binding: 1¼ yards

The finished size is 33" x 34".

Instructions

This quilt is paper pieced using the English paper-piecing method. The size of the hexagon will determine the size of the quilt. A hexagon template has been provided for this quilt. A sheet of hexagon paper has been provided for you to photocopy and paste together to make your pattern. If you want larger hexagons, enlarge the pattern.

1 Using Virginia's quilt idea or a design of your own, use colored pencils to color the flowers and foliage on the grid.

2 Cut a plastic template the size of the hexagon which includes a ¼" seam allowance. Use this plastic template to cut the fabric pieces. If desired, make another plastic template for the flower motifs, but divide the hexagon template into three equal diamond shapes (Remember to add a seam allowance to the diamond shapes before you cut them.) Cut the pieces from assorted fabrics.

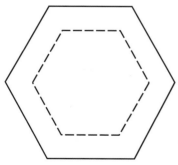

Cut along dashed line for paper pattern.

3 Photocopy and cut out the hexagons for paper piecing using the grid or make your own using the dashed line of the hexagon pattern.

4 Arrange the cut fabric pieces on a flannel design wall or a table. Once you are pleased with the arrangement, begin stitching the pieces together using the English paper-piecing method: Place a paper template in the center of the wrong side of a cut fabric piece. Then turn the seam allowances over and baste through the paper.

Virginia prepares enough pieces to make at least one horizontal row at a time. When basting, insert the needle so the end knot is at the outside edge of the piece. The knot will be easier to remove when you are ready to take out the paper. Use a large, loose backstitch at the end so the basting thread will come out easily. Keep your basted pieces in order, threading them from the bottom of the stack up through the middle, so that you can pull each one off the top of the pile as you need them.

5 To join the pieces, place the first two pieces together with right sides facing, then whipstitch the adjoining edges together starting exactly in the corners. Tack a couple of threads at the corners of each piece and use stitches small enough so that there will be no gaps—about 16 to 18 stitches per side. Begin and end the stitching with a backstitch. Continue adding pieces until the row is complete. The first row is important because it begins to give you ideas for shading. Continue stitching the remaining pieces to the first row, stitching the adjoining edges as you work.

6 Remove the basting stitches and paper pieces after all the sides of each hexagon are stitched. You may use the paper pieces again, if needed.

7 Because of the nature of hexagons, you will have uneven outside edges. With a straight ruler, carefully trim off the extra fabric at the edges of the quilt, keeping a ¼" seam allowance.

8 Finish the quilt following the instructions on page 14. This quilt was hand quilted by stitching ⅛" away from each flower motif to enhance the flower design.

(See page 2 for photocopy permission of page 53.)

Country Garden

by Raedean Beckner

I collect old pictures of cottages and one of my
favorites is an embroidered cottage from the
1930s. I wanted to re-create the picture using
hexagons, so I started playing with the shape,
and the quilt you see emerged. I started piecing
on March 7 and finished the quilting on May 7.
Many of my friends contributed fabric samples to
the total 667 hexagons of different prints pieced in
the quilt. Marge Dobbs of Bend, Oregon, whom I
met at the Sisters Quilt Show in 1994, sent me her
1½"-square fabric samples. When I ran out of fabric halfway
through the project, my sister, Jody Egerman of Boise, Idaho, sent
me some more. Then my friends Carole Thickstun and Chris Bell also
contributed to the quilt fabrics. Through it all, my husband, Ken, was
learning to cook and luckily, he didn't mind leftovers.

Materials

You will need six hundred and sixty-seven 1½" squares of fabric. Look
at the photo and you will see a variety of lights, mediums, and darks in the
hexagon flower garden. The dark prints comprise approximately 25% of
the design, the medium prints 40%, and the light prints 35%.

- Cottage: 6" x 7"
- Roof: 4" x 5"
- Eves: 4" x 6"
- Fence: 5" x 10"
- Hill (in front of cottage): 3" x 9"
- Windows, Shutters, Door, and
  Trim: assorted scraps to total ⅛
  yard
- Backing and Binding: 1 yard

- Six-strand Embroidery Floss: one
  skein each of black, white, and
  yellow-gold; one skein of two
  shades each of purple and green,
  and four shades each of pink and
  blue
- Cardstock or file cards for
  appliqué patterns
- Spray starch
- Glue stick

The finished size is 18" x 22".

Instructions

Hexagon Piecing Instructions

1 Use the hexagon pattern to make a plastic template. The ⅛" seam allowance is included in the pattern.

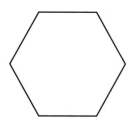

2 Arrange and stack the cut fabric squares into color groups of six or seven pieces. Cut out the hexagons using the template.

3 Using an ⅛" seam allowance, stitch by hand seven fabrics into a circle with the seventh piece in the circle center to create a flower shape. Begin and end with a backstitch.

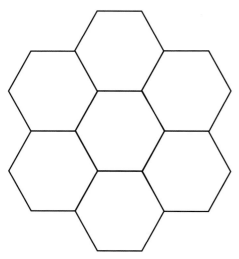

4 Press the seams open and spray starch the shape. Arrange the circle shapes on a flannel design wall. The cottage will overlap the edges of some of the hexagons on the left hand side of the cottage and on the right the hexagons will come over the edge of the cottage. There are 23 hexagons that go across the quilt. Leave the edges loose where the cottage needs to fit in. Once you are pleased with the arrangement, begin stitching the flower hexagons together.

Appliqué Instructions

5 Make two copies of the cottage pattern. Mark the pieces A, B, C, etc. Cut out each piece and glue it to cardstock. Cut out the cardstock templates. Placing the patterns right side down onto the wrong side of the fabrics, cut the shapes from the fabric adding a scant ¼" seam allowance to the edges.

appliqué pattern

wrong side of fabric

6 Spray a little spray starch in a dish. Use your finger or a small paint brush to set the seam allowance. Using the point of the iron, press the seam allowance to the back of the template. Check each fabric shape against the pattern copy. Position the shapes to form the cottage. Start with the back part of the house on the left side of the roof. Pick up the roof and house section with right sides facing to begin stitching. Use a single thread and whipstitch the appliqué pieces together to form the cottage. Begin and end with a backstitch. When you flatten out the two pieces you will have a tight little seam.

7 Press the cottage shape when complete. The cardstock patterns can be removed once the cottage is complete. Use a blind appliqué stitch to add the window and door pieces. Appliqué the cottage to the quilt using a blind stitch.

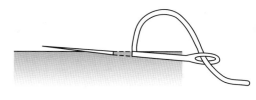

Blind Stitch

Embroidery Instructions

8 Using two strands of embroidery floss, outline all of the cottage details and the fence with a stem stitch.

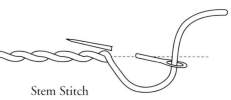

Stem Stitch

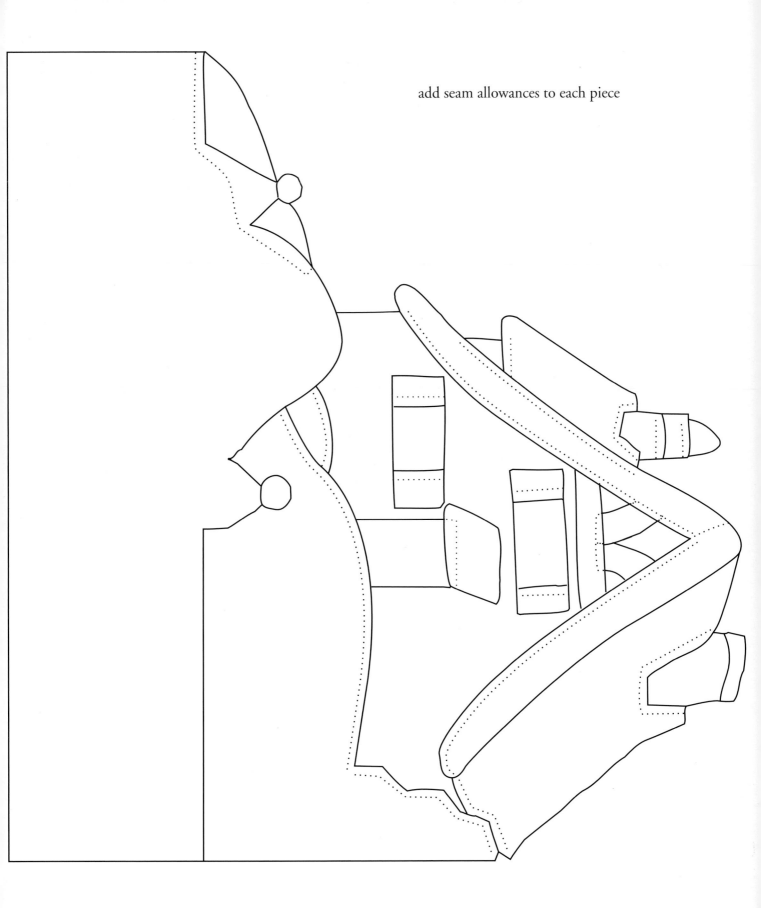

add seam allowances to each piece

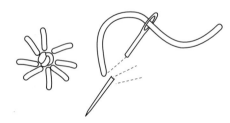

Straight Stitch

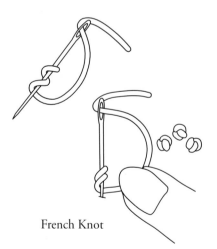

French Knot

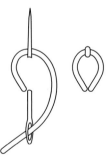

Lazy Daisy Stitch

9 Add flowers to the side of the cottage, in the window box, and above the fence using a Straight Stitch, and French knots for the flowers, and a Lazy Daisy Stitch for the leaves.

10 The cat is outlined with a stem stitch and filled in with straight stitches.

11 Finish the quilt following the instructions on page 14. This quilt was hand quilted by stitching ⅛" away from each flower motif to enhance the flower design.

Chapter 4

Poppy Fields

by Phyllis Smith

The idea for the *Poppy Fields* design was originally developed after viewing a Log Cabin quilt that incorporated a wide range of colors and angles within the strips. Jean Wells, showing me the Log Cabin quilt, liked the checkerboard outline of the square and was able to visualize a fence. But looking at the square, I was able to see a field of poppies. And so the challenge began…

Planning the poppy quilt was fairly typical. I looked through piles of gardening and nature magazines. I located three or four pictures that gave me an idea as to how to approach the quilt design. On a piece of graph paper I drew out the dimensions. Then I sat down with my pictures and color pencils and drew out my idea of a brilliant poppy field, a soft meadow, stately mountains, and blue sky. Being a person who has no faith in my drawing skills, I made the sketch as simple as possible.

Next I searched for the fabrics. I tried to find orange hues in a wide range from rust to peach. Although I was first drawn to the more muted oranges and rusts, I realized that the orange was almost iridescent after study-ing pictures of a California poppy. To depict the bright orange of a California poppy I needed brilliant oranges that were quite bright. It made me smile to see the colors were so wild as I added them to my collection of soft restful col-ors. One of the most important orange fabrics collected was a tie-dyed fabric in which the primary color is orange. This fabric was used as a transition from the poppy field to the meadows because it included a leaf pattern of green with a wide range of tones.

I created a Log Cabin block and then foundation pieced it to muslin. Different fabrics were pieced within some of the strips. This created more angles in the piecing and more interest in the quilt. Some of the blocks are on point while others are straight. As I worked through the assembly of each block I placed it on a blank wall. I auditioned strips of different fabrics until I was pleased with the composition. For this quilt, the fabrics and colors were determined in the design process, but the location of fabrics was decided while I was constructing the blocks. It took a while for the images I had in my mind to emerge. I spent up to 8 hours on some of the blocks, simply trying to re-create my ideas of nature with fabric. Creating the poppies and meadow was more difficult than creating the mountains and sky. The poppies needed inten-sity, whereas the meadow needed substance and blending. The mountains and sky provided a subtle frame for the poppies.

For me, the *Poppy Fields* quilt was a wonderful exercise in creativity. I do believe that we can create beautiful impressions of nature, while enjoying the challenge of awakening the creative process we all have within ourselves.

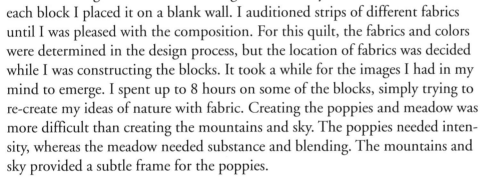

Materials

You will need a variety of prints to total 3 yards for piecing. The blue for the sky comprises approximately 20% of the design, the brown for the mountains 25%, the green for the foliage 30%, and the oranges and yel-lows for the poppies 25%.

- Muslin (foundation): 1⅝ yards
- Backing and Binding 1¾ yards

The finished size is 48½" x 36½". The finished block size is 12" square.

Instructions

1 Cut twelve 14"-square foundation blocks from the muslin. Determine the center of the block and mark it with a pencil. Initially, I planned on a traditional placement of the Log Cabin blocks. However, as these blocks developed, the placement was too rigid so I turned the blocks 90° (on point). The 14" square of muslin was adequate in size to provide for a 12" finished block.

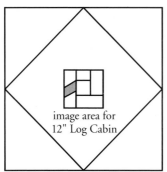

14" square muslin

2 Cut a 2" x 42" strip of each fabric to begin piecing the blocks. Cut additional strips as you need them.

3 The blocks are assembled in a typical Log Cabin method: starting in the center of the muslin with a square and adding the strips in a circular order, stitching and flipping as you work. Press the seams as you work, and add the remaining strips to complete the blocks. The strips in most cases are unique and contain a multitude of fabrics pieced at various angles. Determining which color fabric to use in each strip, which angle, and the variety and size of the pieces was the most challenging part of creating each block. For me, every piece of fabric and every angle was an individual decision.

4 As you complete a block, position it on a flannel design wall. Then put up another piece of muslin and start planning the colors for the next block. This process helps create the natural transitions that form between the blocks.

5 Stitch the blocks together into horizontal rows, and press. Join the rows together: row 1 to row 2 and then row 3. Press.

6 Finish the quilt following the instructions on page 14. This quilt was machine quilted by stitching in the ditch between the blocks and in some of the major seam lines.

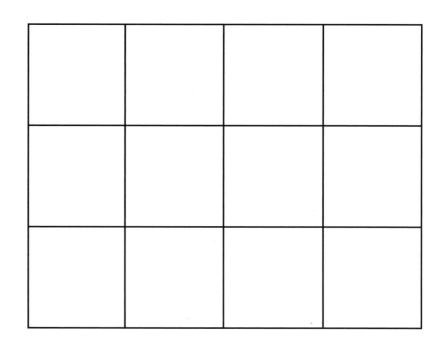

Detail of floral coffee table

Pressed Flower Collages

After collecting and pressing flowers from your garden, you may wonder what to do with them all. Fortunately, there are numerous possibilities: embellishing picture frames, chairs, tables, cards, journals, and keepsake bags. The materials you need for working on wood or thick cardboard boxes are:

• A chair, table, or frame that has a clean surface, either sanded or painted. I like to use latex or acrylic paint on the wood.

• Planatol,® a water-based adhesive, or other glues of this type.

• Varnish in either a gloss medium or matte medium. (Both of these are used in acrylic painting and work well for adhering the flowers and adding a protective layer.)

• Assorted brushes: an old small paintbrush for the glue, a sponge brush if you are painting on wood, and a soft, clean brush for adding the varnish.

• A variety of pressed flowers and foliage.

Optional: Tweezers are very helpful for handling the flowers.

The materials for the cards, journals, and keepsake bags are the same for wood and thick cardboard except that you don't need the varnish. If you wish to protect the cards then you might want to use laminating film. Other options for embellishment would be ribbon or lace.

First determine the flowers you are going to use, and get a basic idea of the arrangement you would like on the surface. Then glue the flowers by either painting the surface you are putting the flowers on or painting the back side of the flower. For the furniture, I painted the wood surface and placed the flowers onto it. For the boxes, cards, journals, and bag, I painted the backs of the flowers. It is a little more tedious to paint the back of the flowers but on the smaller projects it is a better method (the tweezers come in handy for a sticky flower).

For the furniture, painting the surface with the glue is easier because it dries clear and saves time. If you are using a varnish later, let the glue dry overnight. Then the next day carefully paint the varnish over the flowers. One coat of varnish is sufficient for the boxes and the frame, but put on at least three coats for the furniture. Make sure each coat is completely dry before adding the next coat.

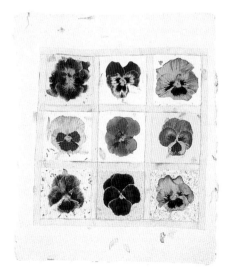

Floral coffee table

Roses

by Ruth Golden Ingham

The night before I started this piece I had been thinking heavily about the design. Just before I went to sleep, I imagined a wooded path with millions of wildflowers covering the ground. Tall, straight tree trunks extended over the view. Yet, while I slept the whole image changed. When I awoke, I could see full blown roses in pinks and reds, and green leaves surrounded everything. So strong was the picture that I jumped out of bed, rushed to the studio, cut a 12½" square of muslin, and designed and foundation pieced the center block.

Over the next few days I created a number of other square and rectangular blocks that would work with the original block. I had to fight the desire to add more and more fabrics. Eventually, I limited my fabric selection and used these fabrics over and over for continuity. This quilt project has become a wonderful learning experience for me.

Materials

You will need a variety of prints to total 2 yards for piecing. The green for the foliage comprises approximately 20% of the design, the reds and pinks for the roses 70%, and yellow 10%.

- Muslin (foundation): 1 yard
- Backing and Binding: 1⅛ yards

The finished size is 24½" x 30½".
The finished block sizes are 4", 6", 8", and 12".

Instructions

1 Cut out the muslin foundation pieces following the quilt illustration. These measurements include ¼" seam allowances.

2 Cut a 2" x 44" strip of each fabric to begin piecing. Cut additional strips as you need them for piecing.

3 This style of foundation piecing is based on the Log Cabin block. Place an odd-shaped piece in the center of the muslin square. Lay a strip of fabric, right sides facing, on one side of the piece. Stitch the pieces together through all three layers. Flip the strip over, press and trim the excess fabric to follow along the edges of the center piece.

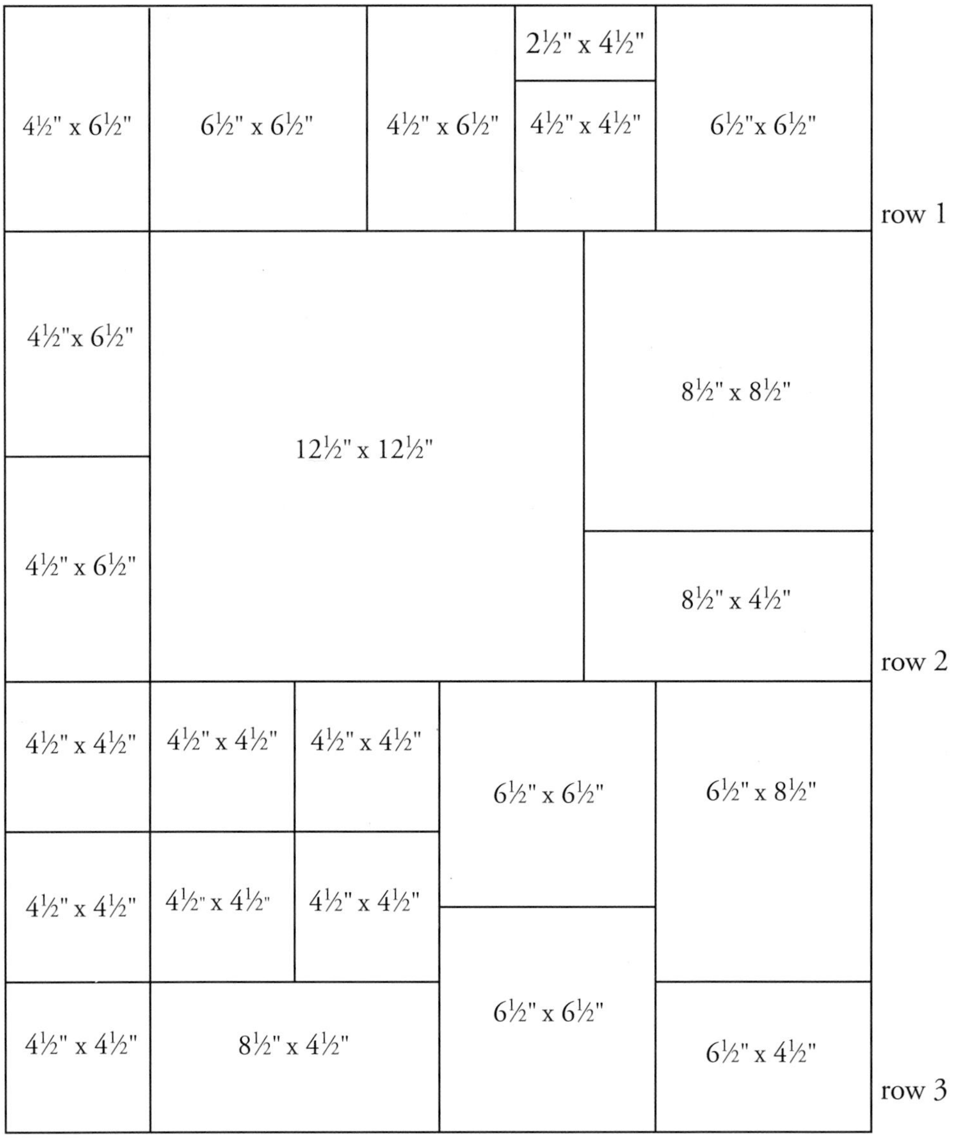

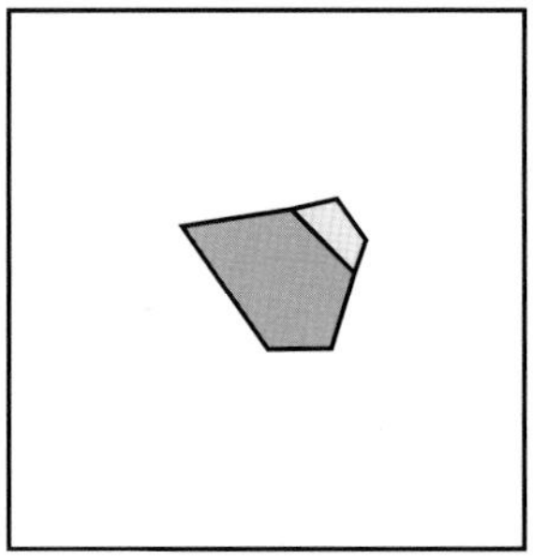

			2½" x 4½"	
4½" x 6½"	6½" x 6½"	4½" x 6½"	4½" x 4½"	6½" x 6½"

row 1

4½"x 6½"				
	12½" x 12½"		8½" x 8½"	
4½" x 6½"			8½" x 4½"	

row 2

4½" x 4½"	4½" x 4½"	4½" x 4½"		
			6½" x 6½"	6½" x 8½"
4½" x 4½"	4½" x 4½"	4½" x 4½"		
			6½" x 6½"	
4½" x 4½"	8½" x 4½"			6½" x 4½"

row 3

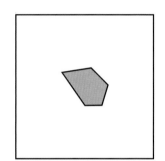

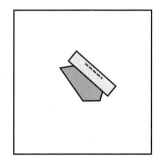

68

4 As you add strips, wedge the shapes by trimming the strip at an angle. This will make the piecing and design look more interesting.

Look closely at the quilt photograph for ideas on shaping the pieces and using color. Note how the tiny bit of very intense lime green and yellow colors enhance the quilt. A wonderful foliage fabric that has dark greens and maroon works as a transition from the rose to the foliage.

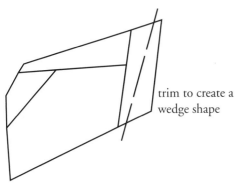

trim to create a wedge shape

5 Arrange the pieces on a design wall. Stitch the blocks together into horizontal rows, and press. Join the rows together: row 1 to row 2, then add row 3.

6 Finish the quilt following the instructions on page 14. This quilt was machine quilted by stitching in the ditch at all the major seam lines.

Sunflowers

by Jean Wells

It is hard to ignore sunflowers—they are so dramatic as they stand above everything else in the garden. Belonging to the daisy family, sunflowers have the same basic shape: their petals radiate from a circular center. When you look at the foliage in a group of sunflowers, some of the leaves stick straight out while some flop over at the tips, creating wedge-like shapes. In other areas, the blue sky appears as a wedge peaking through the leaves. After observing sunflower photographs I had taken last summer, I found that many times a smaller row of darker petals appears next to the center. Although I have been intrigued with sunflowers for a long time, I finally figured out how to set the flowers into a quilt design. Using the same foundation piecing method that Ruth Ingham, one of my students in the Flower Impressions class, was using for her *Roses* quilt, I experimented with a sunflower block and liked the results. Then I adapted the pieced arc from the *Bachelor's Button* quilt and made it a smaller, double arc to create more detail in the petal area. The arcs are hand stitched to the quilt top.

I introduced a transition fabric with the sunflower yellow, foliage greens, and light green of the same value as the sky blue fabrics to join the colors together. Choosing the fabrics for this quilt seemed easier than for the others. Maybe it was because I was training myself to see more possibilities in the fabric itself, and this was the last quilt I did. When I finished the blocks, the quilt top sat for several days with the whole sunflower left intact—I just couldn't bear to cut the flowers apart. Then one morning I went downstairs to work on another project and got the idea to try black for the border, leaving the flower intact. It worked and I felt very euphoric!

Materials

You will need a variety of prints to total 1¾ yards for piecing. The blue for the sky comprises approximately 15% of the design, yellow golds 25%, browns for the sunflowers 5%, and greens 55%.

- Muslin (foundation): 1 yard
- Border and Binding: ⅝ yard
- Backing: 1 yard
- Lightweight tracing paper

The finished size is 28½" x 34½". The grid is a 6" repeat.

Instructions

There are seven arcs that make up the sunflower design. Notice in some of the background areas that blue prints have been used, as well as different greens, to create a feeling that the sky is peaking through the sunflowers. Also, the green fabrics change at the edges of the arc to create an expression of foliage.

Piecing the Arc

1 Trace seven large and seven small arcs onto the tracing paper. Cut the paper patterns on the outer lines.

2 Cut a 1½" x 22" strip from each fabric you will use for the background. Some may be green and a few may be blue to look like the sky. You may need more strips, but you can cut them as needed when you see what colors the quilt needs.

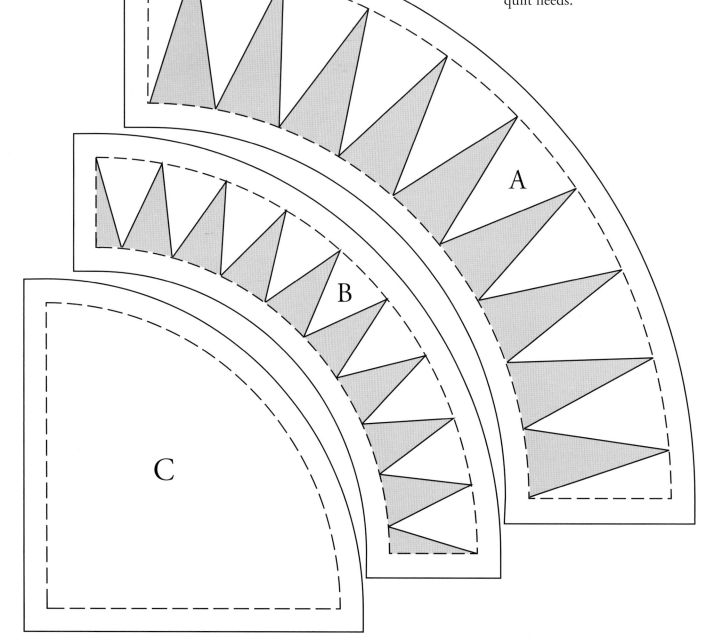

3 Cut a 1¼" x 42" strip from each fabric you will use for the flowers. (I used the same fabric for the outside points on each arc but varied the golds on the background at the inside arc.)

4 Refer to the arc piecing instructions on page 78 and piece the arcs, then set them aside. Finish the remainder of the wedge pieced blocks before piecing the tops of the blocks with arcs. You want to have the arcs placed on the pieced quilt so you will know whether to use foliage fabric or sky.

5 For the sunflower centers, cut seven pieces of muslin using Pattern C. Following the Wedge Foundation Piecing instructions, wedge piece the sunflower centers using brown fabrics.

6 Add pieces to the arc following Step 2-5 of the Setting the Arc instructions on page 80. Clip the inside curve of A.

Wedge Foundation Piecing

This style of piecing resembles crazy quilt blocks, but the work is all done on the sewing machine. These are general instructions. I suggest that you experiment with the technique and sew a couple of practice blocks. I present two different styles for you to try, but I suggest you develop your own style as you work. There is no wrong way to work this technique. You can always cover something you don't like with another wedge. The important aspect of this style of piecing is to vary the shape, and remember that the wedge shape is narrow to wide.

1 Cut two 6½" squares of muslin foundation for your practice blocks. I like to cut my wedges from strips of fabric as I go. Cut the strips about 2½" wide. There is some waste involved, but the leftover pieces may be used on the corners.

2 Method 1 starts with a wedge-cut piece toward the center of the block. First, place a strip of fabric on the edge of #1 right sides together. Stitch through the three layers, and then flip #2 to the right. Press. Trim the excess from #2 following the angle on #1.

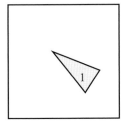

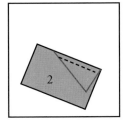

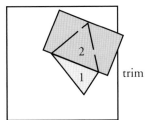

trim

At this time you can trim the right edge of #2 to look like a wedge. You can always trim at this step to shape the pieces. This technique is called "stitch and flip." Follow the numbers in the piecing sequence to complete the sample block. (As you stitch you will find yourself becoming more inventive. This technique is addictive because there is no right or wrong way to piece.)

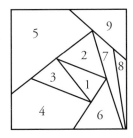

piecing order

Method 2 involves piecing a section that is separate from the foundation, and later adding it to the block. Start with strip #1, and in order add #2, 3, and 4 to the foundation. To make #5, stitch several scrap pieces together. Add this piece to the top of the foundation block. Then add strips #6, 7, 8, and 9 separately.

I think you can see that anything goes. If you don't like an area you pieced, put another strip over the top of it.

the background piecing of the arcs and match them to the wedges. The arcs will be hand stitched in place to the wedge piecing when it is finished. You want the arcs to work with the background composition.

5 To stitch the blocks together, join A, B, and C, and then add to D. Press the pieces. Add E to F and join to the above piece. Join G, H, and I and add to the above piece. Join J, K, and L and add to the side of the above piece. Place an arc on E, F and J. Turn the edge under ¼" and hand stitch in place. Stitch the remaining four arcs together. They will be

stitched to the quilt after the border is attached.

6 For the border, cut two strips of fabric 2½" x 30½" and add to the sides of the quilt. Cut two strips 2½" x 28½" and add to the top and bottom of the quilt.

7 Place the sunflower on the quilt and stitch around the edge as you did for the previous arcs.

8 Finish the quilt following the instructions on page 14. This quilt was machine quilted by stitching in the ditch between the blocks and around the sunflower shapes.

3 Using the quilt illustration as a guide, cut the foundation pieces. The measurements include ¼" seam allowances.

Notice that within the 6" repeat I have combined some of the blocks. This created larger spaces in order to wedge piece. You may choose to divide up the spaces any way you wish. Put them up on the flannel board and place the arcs you have constructed where you think you want them. Look closely at my quilt to identify where the color changes are and then create the impression that you want in your quilt; it doesn't have to look exactly like mine. Decide where the sunflowers will be placed and piece to that area.

4 Start wedge piecing the blocks working to where you have placed the arcs. As you approach an arc, consider the fabrics that you have used in

	A 6½" x 6½"	B 6½" x 6½"	C 6½" x 6½"
L 6½" x 18½"	D 6½" x 18½"		
K 6½" x 6½"	E 12½" x 12½"		F 6½" x 12½"
J 6½" x 6½"	I 6½" x 6½"	H 6½" x 6½"	G 6½" x 6½"

Chapter 5

Bachelor's Buttons

by Jean and Valori Wells

Ten years ago, I threw bachelor's button seeds into my flower bed during the springtime. Each year I let the flowers go to seed and by next spring there are even more. They are some of the first flowers to bloom in the spring and they continue to bloom throughout the summer. Bachelor's buttons are some of my favorite flowers, especially when they mix with the other flowers in the garden to create a myriad of color.

As I observe these flowers, I see small spiky flower shapes with a slim stem and long thin leaves. The New York Beauty arc with its sharp points reminded me of the bachelor's buttons. I made a few of the arcs and varied the colors from bright blue to softer pinks to intense purple just to get the mood of the flowers. Then I had to think about how to set the arc in the block. Originally I was going to use a straight set but realized I would lose the shape of the flower. After a few days of pondering this dilemma I came up with the idea of setting the blocks on point and using a Nine Patch block so I could create more interest within the piecing of the quilt. The Nine Patch design gave me more individual units to vary the fabric choices and create more interest in the quilt.

In the beginning when I was collecting fabric I could not find very many true, light-blue sky mood fabrics, so I had settled on using only one fabric. That seemed appropriate for a while, but then I realized that the sky was too boring. I searched for more light blues, which helped the quilt design. Using a design wall, I would work in an area and then look at it later with a fresh eye. After much dilemma and comments from my quilting friends and my daughter, I started filtering the light fabrics down into the foliage. This really helped the quilt design. Had I gone outside and sat on the ground in front of my flowers, I would have seen this happening.

Detail of *Sunshine and Bachelor's Buttons*

Phyllis Smith, a quilting friend who owns Eastside Gardens in Bend, Oregon, came out to sew with me one day. Toward the end of the day, she said, "It would be really great to scallop the outer edge of the quilt the same shape as the arcs." I had never thought of that, but it is a good example of repetition. Taking the arc shape and repeating it on the border gave the quilt unity. Although this quilt took three months to design, it is a much better quilt since it matured over time. I liken it to the time it takes for a seed to grow to maturity.

Materials

You will need a variety of prints to total 4 yards. The blue of the sky comprises approximately 30% of the design, the light, medium, and dark greens for the foliage 60%, and the assorted floral colors 10%.

- Binding: ⅔ yard
- Backing: 3 yards
- Lightweight tracing paper

The finished size is is 67" x 51". The finished block is 9" square, set on point.

Instructions

Don't piece all of the arcs in the beginning. Wait and see where they will be placed to determine if the background will be sky or foliage and what color is needed for the flowers.

Nine Patch Blocks

1 Cut assorted 3½" squares as needed to create each Nine Patch block. Start working on the design board by arranging each block. This quilt has five Nine Patch blocks across and four down. Form half blocks to fill in around the quilt edges.

2 Construct the Nine Patch blocks as shown.

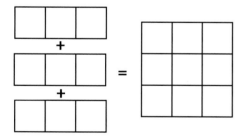

Piecing the Arc

1 Trace the arc pattern onto the tracing paper. Cut out the pattern on the solid lines.

2 Cut a 1¾" x 42" strip from each fabric you will use for the background and the floral points. You may need more strips, but you can cut them as needed when you see what colors the quilt needs.

3 Place the strips right sides together with the background fabric on the top. Place the pattern on the fabric as shown lining up the first seam ¼" from the right-hand side of the cut edges. The top fabric should extend above the paper approximately ¼". Pin in place.

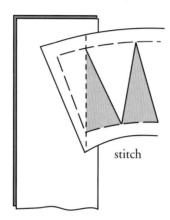

stitch

4 Set the sewing machine stitch length at approximately 18 to 20 stitches to the inch. Stitch through the paper and the fabric on the line, as shown. This is called the "stitch and flip" technique.

5 Flip the flower fabric to the right, over the seam allowances, and finger press.

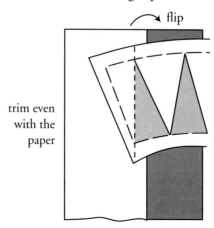

flip

trim even with the paper

Trim off the excess fabric at the top, side, and the bottom, even with the edge of the paper.

6 Select the background fabric and with the pattern facing you, align the background strip underneath the flower point so the raw edge extends ¼" to the right of the stitching line. Make sure the strip extends ¼" above the top of the arc. Pin in place and stitch on the line.

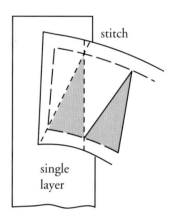

stitch

single layer

7 Fold the paper over and trim the seam allowance to ¼" along the stitching line.

8 Turn the paper so the lines are facing you. Flip the background fabric to the right and finger press. Trim the top and bottom even with the paper. You have now completed a full step. Continue the process until the arc is complete. Always double check which fabric you just used so you don't repeat two background fabrics or two flower fabrics. Press.

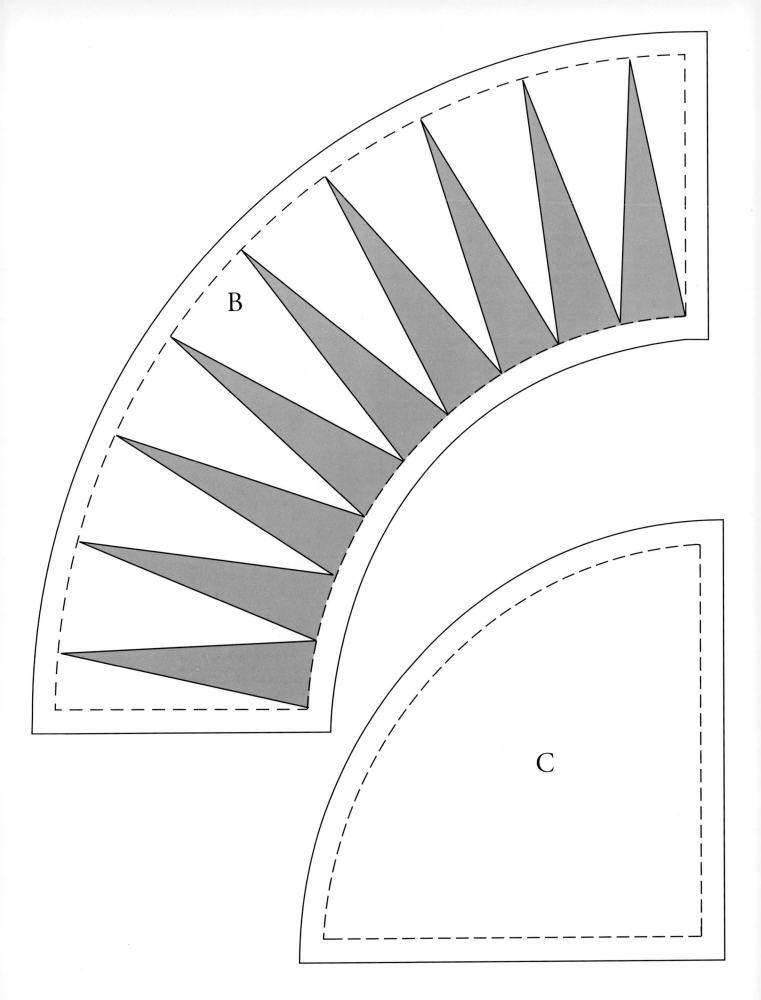

B

C

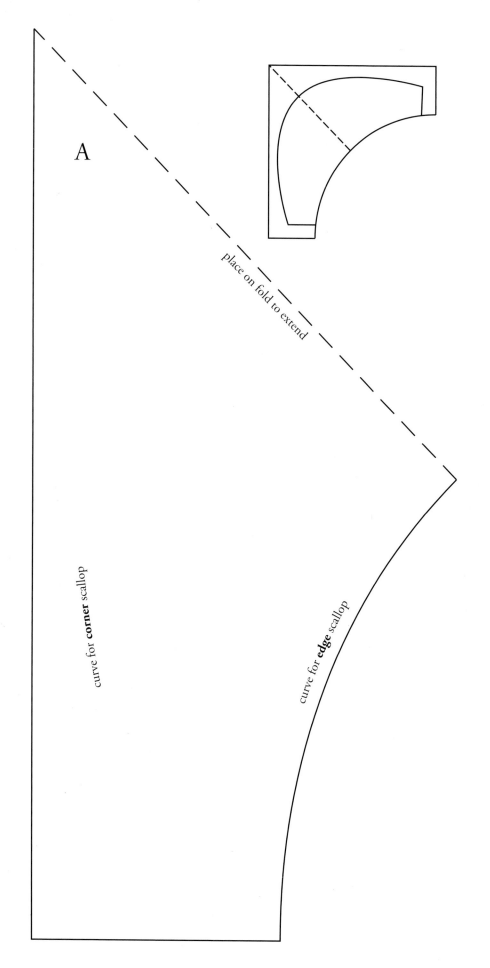

A

place on fold to extend

curve for **corner** scallop

curve for **edge** scallop

Setting the Arc into the Nine Patch Block

1 For the blocks where an arc will be pieced, use Patterns A and C to cut the top and bottom pieces of the block.

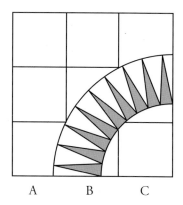

A   B   C

2 Mark the center of the curved edge of A and the arc B with a pin. Clip the curved edge of A every ¼" about ⅛" in from the edge. It is important to be consistent with the clipping.

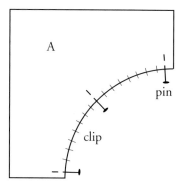

A

pin

clip

3 Match the center of the arc B to A at the pins, and then pin the pieces together. Align the straight edges of each piece at the ends, and pin together.

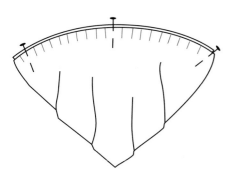

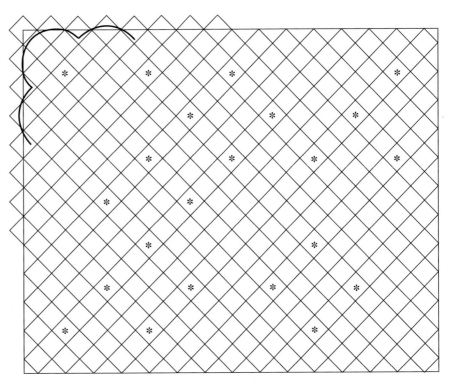

4 At this point you always wonder if this is really going to fit together. But it does if you stitch at exactly ¼" from the edge. Stitch the pieces together slowly, repositioning the block in front of you about every 1½". Just remember that when the patterns were drafted they fit together so if you stitch at ¼" seam allowance they will fit. Do not stitch over pins. Press the seams toward A.

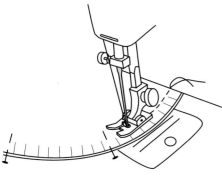

5 Add C to the arc following the same process in Steps 2-4, but you will be clipping the curve on C. Press the seam toward C. Carefully remove the paper pattern. A straight pin helps to grab it. Press the completed block.

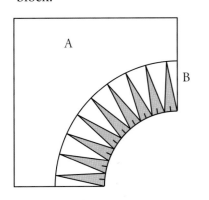

Quilt Construction

1 Stitch the blocks together in diagonal rows: join row 1 to row 2, etc. Press.

2 Trim the points off around the edge of the quilt if you are not going to scallop them.

3 To scallop the edge of the quilt, make a template as shown on Pattern A. Pencil all of the scallops on the quilt before you cut. You may have to adjust here and there to make them work.

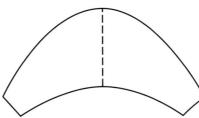

placement of template for scalloped edge

4 If you choose to scallop the edges, cut the binding strips on the bias. Cut the strips

1¾" x 42". You will need a total length of 300". Join the strips together, and then fold them in half matching the long edges. Press. Stitch the binding to the quilt following the instructions on page 15. When the binding is turned to the back, take a small tuck in the dip on each scallop.

5 Finish the quilt following the instructions on page 14. This quilt was first machine quilted between the Nine Patch blocks. Then a long leaf design resembling the bachelor's button leaves was traced randomly along the bottom of the quilt.

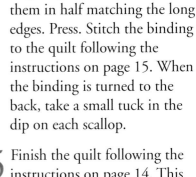

Using the leaf pattern I worked my way up the quilt to create a mood of foliage. Then the flower colors were stitched in the arcs.

Sunshine & Bachelor's Buttons

by Cindy Uttley

I loved the blue and green fabrics in Jean's quilt and I was intrigued by the setting: Nine Patches on point with New York Beauties set in. Also, I was drawn to the design-as-you-go method of designing a quilt from a palette of fabrics. The notion of the quilt taking on a life of its own seemed more significant with this style than a traditional quilt, and it was more challenging.

As I thought through the sketch and my palette, I remembered a snapshot of a quilt from the International Quilt Show in Houston, Texas. The quilter had successfully depicted shadows. I wondered if I could do the same. The idea grew and developed as I looked at my fabrics: better to attempt areas of greater light, warmer yellow-greens in the light areas and bluer greens in the "shaded" areas of the design.

I came across a magazine picture of densely planted hyacinths with a few yellow tulips sprinkled randomly among them. What if I "sprinkled" yellow among the bachelor's buttons? I sketched the design, then tried adding a sense of depth and perspective. Could I change the scale so there are smaller bachelor's buttons towards the top? As I thought about the measurements, I realized that nine is a multiple of three. What if I changed the 9" Nine Patches to 6" instead? That was it! I reduced the New York Beauty arc pattern by 20% and had to draft a new A and C to fit in the 6" block.

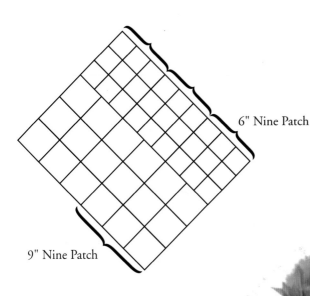

6" Nine Patch

9" Nine Patch

I started constructing the quilt in the lower right-hand corner. When I would get stuck with a design problem, it really helped to have another quilter's input. (At this stage it was most helpful to have our class.) We helped each other in class throughout the difficult decision-making times. I had a hard time finishing the design—Jean didn't want me to tweak it to death. But I think I so enjoyed the adventure that I didn't want it to end. Once the piecing was done, it was a month before I could complete the quilt. For the quilting stitches, I think less is better in this case and I only machine stitched in the ditch. I may go back later and do a small amount of quilting in the background areas of the New York Beauties so the spikes will stand out more.

This whole process has stretched my imagination and given me new courage and confidence to try new styles of quilting.

Pansies

by Jean Wells

After the crocus and daffodils have bloomed, my pansies come along next. Most of them winter fairly well, but I always look forward to purchasing some new colors. This year my friend Phyllis, who owns Eastside Gardens in Bend, Oregon, got in an antique variety with ruffled edges and multicolored petals. They are beautiful. When the pansies are in full bloom, I like to press them between the pages of a telephone book. During one of my flower gathering times, I tossed the flowers into a round basket. (I pick the pansies often to keep new ones coming.) They were so colorful: oranges touching purples and blues and burgundies surrounded by multifaceted yellow blooms. I kept the picture in my mind and designed this quilt to capture the mood of the flowers.

To make the flower petal patterns, I actually traced around the petals, then enlarged the shapes. By following the observation process of looking closely at the flower, I was able to come up with the simple shapes. The centers on the flowers are detailed with straight stitches of embroidery thread. Since pansy

foliage is very dark green and lush, I made the background more interesting by strip piecing several greens together, and then cutting it apart and placing it on the foundation.

Materials

- Green scrap fabrics: 1½ yards total
- Multicolored scrap fabrics for pansies: 1 yard total
- Muslin (foundation): ¾ yard
- Six-strand embroidery floss in a variety of colors for flower centers
- Backing and Binding: 1 yard
- Optional: freezer paper for appliqué

The finished size is 22" x 34".

Instructions

1 Cut a variety of 1¼" to 2" wide green fabric strips 42" long. Stitch them together until you have a piece that measures 36" x 42".

2 Cut a 22" x 34" piece of muslin for the foundation.

3 To create interest for the background, cut up the green pieced fabric strips into large sections with opposing seams. Allow for a ¼" seam allowance on all the edges. The illustration shows a possible arrangement of the background fabric. Stitch together and baste to the muslin foundation.

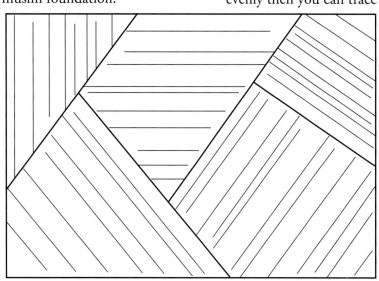

4 Using the photograph as a guide, note how the pansies are formed. Use the patterns provided to create the petal shapes (the seam allowance is <u>not</u> included) and cut them from the assorted fabrics. Position the petals on the background fabric, and then baste the petals using long stitches that will be easy to pull out. Appliqué one petal at a time, as described.

5 Needle-turn appliqué uses the needle to pull under the edge as you move around the appliqué shape. To use this method, only turn under a scant ¼" at the edge. Bring the needle up through the fabric and just barely catch a couple threads of the appliqué fabric. Put the needle directly back down into the background fabric. Carry the needle under the wrong side of the fabric about ⅛" for the next stitch.

If you have trouble turning under the edge of the fabric evenly then you can trace the appliqué shape on plastic coated freezer paper. Cut out the petals from the paper and press the wax side to the top of the pansy fabric. Cut ⅛" beyond the paper pattern for the seam allowance. Turn under the edge of the fabric using the paper as a guide. Tear off the paper when you are done.

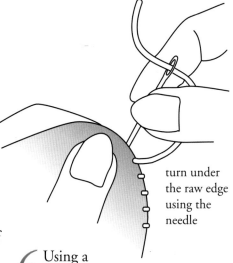

turn under the raw edge using the needle

6 Using a Size 8 embroidery needle and two strands of floss, take short, medium, and long straight stitches from the center then radiate out to highlight the pansy design. You may want to mix a couple of thread colors. Look closely at the photograph of the pansies to get ideas for the centers.

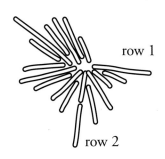

row 1

row 2

7 Finish the quilt following the instructions on page 14. This quilt was machine quilted around the pansy shapes.

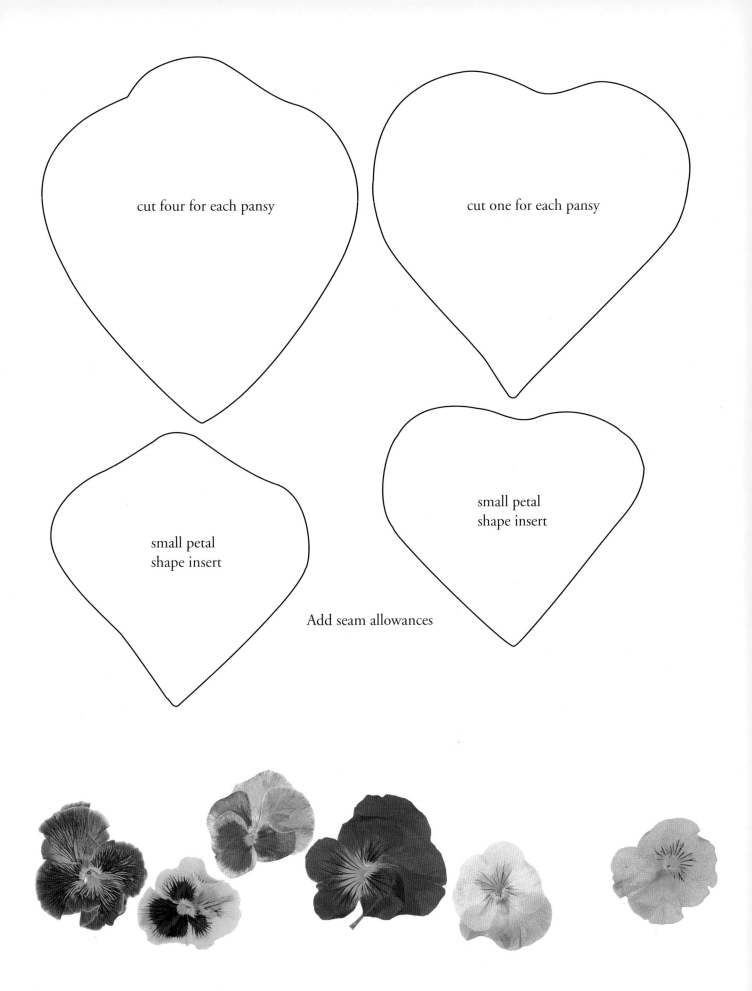

cut four for each pansy

cut one for each pansy

small petal
shape insert

small petal
shape insert

Add seam allowances

Floral and Herbal Baths

After a long day of pulling weeds in your garden, a nice relaxing bath is wonderful. By adding herbs and flowers, fresh or dried, to your bath you can unwind for a restful sleep, soothe and relax your muscles, invigorate and stimulate your circulation, or simply enjoy their aroma. The following list of herbs and flowers can be used in a bath bag.

Bath Herbs and Flowers

Chamomile: soothing and relaxing, calms the nerves

Comfrey leaf, flower and root: invigorating, rejuvenating, cleansing as an astringent and emollient.

Honeysuckle: aromatic, softens the skin

Jasmine: softens and cleanses the skin

Lavender: natural disinfectant, stimulates the complexion, aromatic with a clean refreshing scent, astringent

Lemon Balm: relaxing

Marigold: stimulant and diaphoretic

Mint (all kinds): invigorating, restorative, stimulant

Rose petals: cleansing, softening, astringent, soothing fragrance

Rosemary: diaphoretic and an astringent healer

Sage: aromatic and cleansing

Strawberry leaves: astringent

Thyme: aromatic and antiseptic

Violets: aromatic

Wintergreen: aromatic

Yarrow: diaphoretic, cleansing and soothing

Bath Recipes

These recipes are very easy and you can either use a bath bag or make an infusion of the fresh or dried herbs and flowers. Taking a bath with just a single herb, such as lavender, is as wonderful as mixing a variety of the herbs and flowers. When using dried herbs and flowers, it is good to mix a large quantity and put in an air tight jar so you don't have to mix the recipe every time you wish to take a bath. You don't even have to take a bath—simply rub the bag gently over your body in the shower. Experiment with different combinations or herbs and you'll soon find taking baths is very enjoyable.

Use equal amounts of each ingredient in the following recipes.

For a simple, soothing and cleansing bath use jasmine flowers, rose petals, and comfrey.

To smooth and soothe the skin use thyme (antiseptic), comfrey (emollient), lavender (astringent), and mint (aromatic).

For rejuvenating and regenerating, use lavender, rosemary, peppermint, comfrey root, lemon thyme, and rose petals.

For an all around good bath, use lavender, rosemary, comfrey, and rose petals.

These recipes are bases for using the bath bag.

Soothing Bath

Add 2 tablespoons of medium oatmeal and 2 tablespoons of herb mixture of your choice into a bath bag. Rub the bag gently over your body while relaxing in the bath.

Moisturizing Bath

Add a few drops of almond oil into your bath water. Use a bath bag filled with your choice of herbs to rub over your body. Your skin will begin to feel and look smoother.

Soap Bath Bag

Add 2 tablespoons of medium oatmeal, 1 tablespoon of grated, unscented, basic herbal soap and 2 tablespoons of your choice of herb mixture. Use the bag in the bath to gently wash your body.

Bath Bag Instructions

Materials Needed

6" x 16" loosely woven cotton fabric
⅔ yard of ⅛"-wide ribbon

1 Cut a 6" x 16" piece of prewashed cotton fabric that is loosely woven.

2 Fold 2" of the short ends toward the center of the right side of the fabric, and press. Stitch the edges as shown (leaving a ½" opening). Turn right sides out and press.

4 Cut the ribbon in half. Using a safety pin, attach the pin to one end of the ribbon, and thread through the opening, as shown. Tie the ends together. Thread the second length of ribbon through from the opposite direction.

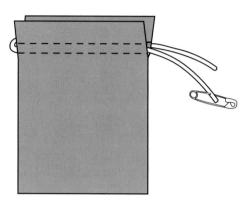

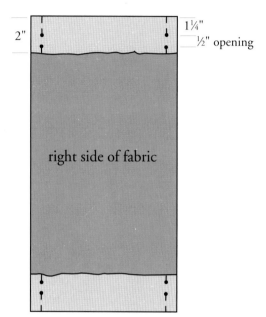

2" 1¼"
½" opening

right side of fabric

3 Clip the seam allowance at the bottom of the stitches as shown. Topstitch 1¼" down from the folded edge. Topstich a second row ½" below the first to form a casing.

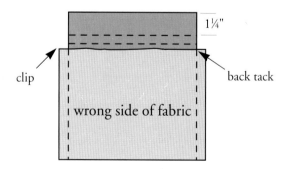

1¼"

clip back tack

wrong side of fabric

Fold in half, right sides together and stitch the side seams. Back tack. Turn to right side.

Remembrance of Summer

by Valori Wells

Embers
Glowing in the fireplace
Warming my body from the brisk air.
A sweet tantalizing aroma of Russian tea.
Through the windows of the this warmth
    and comfort
A white blanket covers our mother earth.
Slick, smooth icicles diminish and change
in the December rays.
Layers of snowflakes arch the branches
of mighty ponderosas.
Sparkling limbs of bare aspens
surround a sleeping pond.
Birdhouses are still and the flower beds
    covered.
The playful songs and brilliant colors of
    summer
Only remembered.

In full bloom every flower is admired.
Every bed is carefully thought out.
The sturdy golden sunflowers
drink from the nourishing sun.
Rows of brilliant white daisies
sway in the breeze.
The sweet fragrance of lavender
stirs the senses.
Delicate pansies and plentiful bachelor's buttons
Vivid poppies and gentle roses
Expectant snapdragons and precious
    wildflowers
Remain clear in my mind.
Every color
glowing and bright.
Every shape
unique.

Every scent
stimulating and meaningful.
Bundled in a quilt
cozy and warm.
Enormous snowflakes
lining the ground.
All my thoughts
stirring memories.
The damp grass
between my toes.
Green and bright
so full of life.
Nourishing soil
willing to give life
coating my hands.
The July sun
beating down.
A slight breeze
cooling my body.

Oh, when weather is warm and flowers
    are blooming
My companions of winter will be forgotten.
The coaxing fireplace
Best seat in the house
will just be dark and unused,
Filled with reminders of winter.
Windows and doors that protect
will be wide open filling the house with summer
    scents.
But
The fire is crackling
the windows are shut
and the fresh aroma of cut greens fills the air.
I dream of my summer paradise
cradling a basket overflowing with nature's
    creations
Exploring,
examining
every petal,
leaf,
shape,
color,
scent.

REMEMBRANCE OF SUMMER

EMBERS
GLOWING IN THE FIREPLACE
WARMING MY BODY FROM THE BRISK AIR
A SWEET TANTALIZING AROMA OF RUSSIAN TEA.
THROUGH THE WINDOWS OF THIS WARMTH AND COMFORT
A WHITE BLANKET COVERS OUR MOTHER EARTH.
SLICK, SMOOTH ICICLES DIMINISH AND CHANGE
IN THE DECEMBER RAYS.
LAYERS OF SNOWFLAKES ARCH THE BRANCHES
OF MIGHTY PONDEROSAS.
SPARKLING LIMBS OF BARE ASPENS
SURROUND A SLEEPING POND.
BIRDHOUSES ARE STILL AND THE FLOWERBEDS COVERED.
THE PLAYFUL SONGS AND BRILLIANT COLORS OF SUMMER
ONLY REMEMBERED.

COLOR,
SCENT.

AND CREATIVITY FLOURISHED
MY PLACE
WHERE NATURE IS EVERYTHING.

My sanctuary…
a trickling waterfall
replenishing its quaint pond.
A group of aspens
thriving from the bank.
A faithful, old ponderosa
casting a shadow.
A ring of colors
covering its trunk.
A garden in bloom
unfolded and exposed.
A cushion of green
to cool and comfort.

A place
where the beauty of summertime can be
preserved for winter.
Every petal and every leaf
filling a basket to be admired for years.
A place
where dreams begin
and end.
Where passion ignites
and creativity flourishes.
My place
Where nature is everything.

About the Authors

Jean and Valori Wells are a mother and daughter team that have combined their talents to create *Everything Flowers.* Twenty-two year old Valori is an art student majoring in photography at Pacific Northwest College of Art in Portland, Oregon. Her love of flowers has been the mainstay for her creativity in college, whether it be writing a poem, creating a block print, pressing flowers for the cover of a handmade paper book, or handpainting a photograph. Valori has always worked in a creative environment. She grew up in a household full of quilts, wearable art, and floral projects, in addition to participating in developing the ever-expanding outdoor garden at her family home.

Jean Wells has been writing books and magazine articles for sixteen years, in addition to running her successful quilt shop, The Stitchin' Post, for twenty-one years in the small mountain community of Sisters, Oregon. The store was recently chosen as one of the top ten quilting shops in America by *American Patchwork and Quilting Magazine.* A talented quilter, Jean seems to always find inspiration and pass it on to others. Her latest accomplishments include designing a line of fabric called Pine Brook with P&B Textiles, and appearing on several televised quilting programs. Jean continues to teach quilting in her shop as well as the United States and abroad.

Bibliography

Keen, Mary. *Gardening with Color*. New York: Random House, 1991.

Midda, Sara. *In and Out of the Garden*. New York: Workman Publishing, 1981.

Martin, Tovah. *Tasha Tudor's Garden*. Boston: Houghton Mifflin Company, 1994.

Murray, Elizabeth. *Monet's Passion*. San Francisco: Pomegranate Artbooks, 1989.

Prittie, Joni. *The Crafter's Garden*. New York: Meredith Press, 1993.

Proctor, Rob. *Country Flowers*. New York: Harper Collins Publishers, 1991.

Tudor, Tasha. *The Private World of Tasha Tudor*. Boston: Little, Brown and Company, 1992.

Sources

Listed below are products that have been mentioned in the text. Art supply stores, craft stores, quilt shops, and fabric stores are the best places to find these products. My suggestion is to use the information below and call your local area shops until you find what you are looking for. My retail quilt shop, The Stitchin' Post, PO Box 280, Sisters, OR (503) 549-6061 does carry the quilt related supplies listed.

Aleene's, Division of Artis, Inc.: Tacky glue®, Hot Stitch®
(craft glue that dries clear, paper-backed adhesive)

EZ International: EZ Stitch-Thru tear-away paper
(tear-away paper for paper piecing arcs)

SPPS: Triangle Paper for Quilters
(half-square triangle grid paper—specify finished size)

Binney & Smith, Inc.: Liquitex® acrylic in gloss medium
(varnish to apply over pressed flowers)

Planatolwerk W. Hesselmann: Planatol®
(glue that dries clear to use with pressed flowers)

E.E. Schenck: Creative Grid®
(2"-wide gridded flannel for design boards)

Skydyes, Mickey Lawler
(hand-painted and dyed fabrics)

Other Books by Jean Wells

Buttonhole Stitch Appliqué
Patchwork Quilts Made Easy with Rodale Press

For a complete list of books by C&T Publishing, write for a free catalog: C&T Publishing, P.O. Box 1456, Layfayette, CA 94549 1(800) 284-1114